Stir it up

A celebration of Scotland's food and culture,
past and present,
in recipes compiled by Yes Berwickshire
with cover and drawings by
Eric Ritchie and
introduction by Lesley Riddoch.

Edited by Dorothy Bruce

Twinlaw

First Published in Great Britain 2018
by Twinlaw Publishing
Kirkcairn, Westruther, Gordon
Scottish Borders TD3 6NE

A CIP catalogue record for this title is available
from the British Library

ISBN: 978-1-9164558-0-1

www.twinlawpublishing.co.uk

YesBerwickshire

Yes Berwickshire would like to thank all those who contributed to this cookery book – Eric, Kathi, Helen, Irene, Lindsay, Liz, Rick, Lyn, Toby, Maree, Mary, Molly, Pete, Terry, Alex, Bethan, Jean, Russell and Dorothy – not forgetting Campbell for his financial wizardry, Eric Ritchie for his amazing artwork, and Lesley Riddoch for her introduction.

Facebook: YesBerwickshire
Twitter: @YesBerwickshire

Lesley Riddoch is a broadcaster, journalist and author who has recently worked with Phantom Power Films to produce fascinating insights into two of Scotland's northerly neighbours.
NATION 1 Faroe Islands - the connected nation
https://tinyurl.com/y6unur5z
NATION 2 Iceland - the extreme nation -
https://tinyurl.com/y7g9m9qz

Do cookery and politics mix?

Lesley Riddoch

Do cookery and politics mix?

Not really, and that surely is the beauty of food.

Even the keenest independence campaigner needs a break and the Yes Berwickshire cookery book offers that in lipsmackin' style. Stir it up let's you flip through recipes by the great, good and the awfy keen - raising money for Scotland's independence campaign, and promoting a 'soft' message about change along the way.

After all, fish and chips used to win the battle hands down as Scotland's most popular dish. Now it gets a run for its money by Chicken Tikka Masala – created decades back in the kitchen of a Glasgow Indian restaurant. Who would have guessed that folk who once worshipped the mince pie would soon be supping all kinds of far eastern cuisine and loving them all?

The good news is that Scotland's national palate is more adaptable than we think – and our traditional dishes healthier than many imagine. Old favourites like porridge are highly recommended by doctors and dieticians across the world, tackling the threat of diabetes with slow release carbs and Scottish staples like raspberries and black pudding are often described as super foods.

The point is that food preferences, like political cultures change slowly over time, influenced by the folk and traditions that make up modern Scotland. So this wee book includes recipes from north and south of the border and from countries in which contributors have travelled or were born and brought up.

There's also a very brief 'story' about each recipe. So even if you are slightly challenged in the art of cooking (like myself), there are tales woven through the ingredients to keep you hooked.

That's partly because *Stir it up* was inspired by a storyteller and author – Isobel Christian Johnstone, the wife of Walter Scott's publisher. She was a Borders lass, editor of *Tait's Edinburgh Magazine*, early feminist and by all accounts a feisty woman with a great sense of humour. In *Meg Dods' Cookery*, Johnstone produced a pot pourri of recipes and writing, hoping that her use of fictional characters like Walter Scott's innkeeper in St. Ronan's Well might "direct attention to that which [readers] may consider a vulgar and unimportant art." A wee introduction by Sir Walter didnae harm sales either.

In *Meg Dods' Cookery*, Isobel Christian Johnstone highlights how the steam revolution (which started in Scotland) made travel and the movement of foodstuffs from across the globe much easier, so that "spiceries" and fruit, once considered luxuries, were finally obtainable by "the industrious even among the working classes." Just like modern Scots today, Ms Christian Johnstone was perky, socially conscious and outward looking and her recipes were influenced by cooking styles in England, France, India, the ports of the Hanseatic League, the Netherlands, Italy and Scandinavia.

Now, almost two hundred years later, folk like myself and the rest of the volunteers at Nordic Horizons are re-exploring Scotland's forgotten Nordic links and Yes Berwickshire is gamely recreating a nineteenth century literary and culinary tradition.

Braw. I hope you enjoy leafing through and creating the much-loved dishes of Scotland and beyond.

Scotland – a world-renowned brand

Scotland has a well recognised brand when it comes to food and drink, a brand that signifies quality, and prompts visions and stories of our history. A brand is more than a name and a fancy logo. A brand encompasses tradition, hopes, aspirations, what the product does for you and says about you as a person. Scotland's name has long been synonymous around the world with premium quality products.

It has become the norm for supermarkets to indicate Scottish produce by a saltire on the packaging so those who prefer to buy local produce can do so. But recently we have seen a change with Scottish produce branded, along with produce from other parts of the UK, with a union flag. Does this matter? Yes, it does. If the Scottish brand is lost or weakened we will lose market share. If we lose market share we lose revenue and our economy will be hit. Even tourism could be impacted as visitors come to Scotland to enjoy our scenery, history and also our home-produced food. Our visitors already spend almost £1 billion every year on food and drink, supporting local producers.

Weaker demand will affect rural communities resulting in loss of jobs and the closure of producers and businesses that add value to local products by turning raw ingredients like salmon into world-renowned smoked salmon. Products such as Scotch Beef and Scottish Farmed Salmon account for around £700 million in sales.

The Scottish Government has estimated that EU Protected Food Name status, on average, increases a product's value by 2.23 times. Scotland has currently fourteen Protected Food Names out of eighty-six registered in the UK (whisky comes under a different Geographical Indication status):
• Traditional Ayrshire Dunlop Cheese • Orkney Scottish Island Cheddar • Stornoway Black Pudding • Scottish Wild Salmon • Shetland Lamb • Orkney Beef • Orkney Lamb • Scottish Farmed Salmon • Scotch Lamb • Scotch Beef • Arbroath Smokie • Native Shetland Wool • Teviotdale Cheese (not in production) • Bonchester Cheese (not in production)

After Brexit these products could lose their Protected Status. Indeed, in the recent Canada/Japan/South Korea/EU talks, the UK government didn't apply for protection for any agricultural products and foodstuffs. Whisky has wider protection, though American spirit producers have made clear they intend to call their whiskey 'Scotch'. This would be devastating not only for our whisky industry, our largest food and drink export that garners a worlwide reputation for quality and tradition, but also for our economy.

This isn't an issue that applies only to Scotland. Loss of brand identity, with it subsumed into a bland UK brand, is an issue for food and drink producers, farmers and horticulturalists in all the UK countries. Yes Berwickshire wants to see our distinctive Scottish branding retained so we can grow the market for the produce from our farmers, fishermen, and food and drink industry, protecting local jobs and livelihoods.

Scotland is on a Journey

Scotland is on a journey. You can see it in the pages of this book. That journey is a political, cultural and culinary journey where we still hold, tenuously in some cases, fast in others, to our traditional past but at the same time embrace the new of our present.

Some recipes here are traditional, like stovies, still liked and made regularly; others, like haggis bites, are an update on traditional fare; others again are new from around the world – though often it's a Scottish take on the dish. Culture and cooking evolve with the times – that's why fish and chips are no longer rated as Scotland's favourite food, their place taken by curry.

Traditional Scottish recipes are often surprising. Just flick through a copy of *Meg Dods' Cookery: Cook and Housewife's Manual*, mentioned by Lesley Riddoch in her introduction. In it you will find that then (our eleventh edition* was published in 1864), as now, cooking was shaped by new inventions and cultural and political events, with the author remarking that it was pleasant to hear of the working classes now able to season their gruel and rice with nutmeg or cassia (an inferior kind of cinnamon), whilst she bemoans the still high cost of sugar.

In a chapter on Bills of Fare the author notes that a first course should contain mainly English dishes while the second should be French dishes, with putrid game no longer admired, and fish being more simply cooked. Fat puddings and very rich cakes and pies have given way to lighter dishes of creams, jellies, caramelised fruits and compotes. Don't be fooled though, for courses are not one dish as we know today, but a whole range of dishes. The third course is not merely a dessert but game, pastry, confectionary, vegetables, salads dressed in the French way as well as a range of sweet dishes.

Cheese and a fresh salad, and sliced cucumber are served as a third course "in respectable English families, who do not affect foreign manners." Finger glasses of course precede the dessert.

Another treasure of traditional recipes is *The Scots Kitchen** by F Marian McNeill, journalist, traveller and authority on Scottish folklore and cooking who also wrote *The Silver Bough*, a four-volume study of Scottish folklore. Annette Hope in *A Caledonian Feast** quotes Jean Anthelme Brillat-Savarin, the French lawyer and politician who gained fame as an epicure and gastronome, saying: 'The fate of nations depends on the way they eat.' In producing this volume the members of Yes Berwickshire are following in notable footsteps.

Wars and rationing took a toll on the foods we could put on our tables, but since joining the European Union in 1973 our diets have changed dramatically – they've become more European with us regularly eating garlic, aubergines, courgettes, pasta, pizza, calamari, salami, and a vast range of different cheeses. You can see the change through the recipes in this book.

Package holidays to Europe saw us returning with new tastes

and an interest in experimenting with strange ingredients and new-fangled recipes. New people have come to Scotland to linger and stay, swelling our population. New people and new culinary influences mean Scotland has a growing, vibrant population, and a culture with a strongly beating heart.

Sadly, Brexit will impact on that, diminish it, make the heart skip more than a few beats, raising questions about our future, our links with other peoples and cultures. But reacting to events by retreating to the past is never entirely possible, and hopefully we will continue, even if at a slower pace and on a road more winding and bumpy, on our journey towards making Scotland the sort of country we want ourselves and our families to live in.

This book is a celebration of Scotland's food and culture, past and present. It has echoes of the traditional Scotland and Borders of the past, of Meg Dods and Marian McNeill, charting our culinary journey to the present where, as in times past, we again embrace new foods and cultures to enrich our own, adding a soupçon of spice to our lives. Without that journey, that embracing of the new, culture, like an unspoken language, shrivels and dies. So let's continue to welcome the new.

The Yes Berwickshire Team

Meg Dods' Cookery: The Cook and Housewife's Manual: A practical system of modern domestic cookery and family management, By Mistress Margaret Dods of the Cleikum Inn, St Ronan's, Eleventh Edition Revised, Edinburgh: Oliver and Boyd, Tweeddale Court, London: Simpkin, Marshall and Co., 1864 (first pub. 1826)

The Scots Kitchen: Its Lore & Recipes, F Marian McNeill, Blackie & Son Ltd, Glasgow and London, Second edition 1963

A Caledonian Feast, Annette Hope, Grafton Books, 1989

Contents

Contents continued

Contents continued

Sections

The cookbook has been divided into colour-coded sections to make it easy for busy cooks to find the section and the recipe they want.

SOUPS

SALADS

SNACKS

FISH

MAIN COURSES

VEGETABLES

SWEETS

BAKING

TREATS

PRESERVES & RELISHES

DRINKS

Lettuce Soup

Every week in the newspaper then called *The Glasgow Herald* I enjoyed the recipes from "Green Gerry", writing from what was called the City Croft.

These recipies were always illustrated with a witty little cartoon. I often wondered where in the city was this fertile oasis that produced healthy vegetables unaffected by smoke and pollution. I never did find out but I enjoyed the humour and the Lettuce Soup recipe.

Ingredients

- 1 lb of lettuce leaves (iceberg, red salad, all-year-round)
- 2 tablespoons butter
- 1 tablespooon diced onion
- 2 tablespoons flour
- 8 fluid ozs chicken stock
- ¾ teasoon salt
- ¼ teaspoon paprika
- A little grated Parmesan

Method

1. Cook the lettuce leaves and drain.
2. Put through a blender.
3. Put into a saucepan, add butter and sauté for 3 minutes.
4. Add onion and stir until blended.
5. Gradually stir in the flour and the chicken stock.
6. Season with salt and paprika.
7. Serve with a sprinkling of Parmesan

Ramen

Ramen is a very popular noodle soup in Japan. There are two main components in Ramen: noodles and soup. The noodles are called Chinese style noodles or Chuka-men but these are nothing like Chinese noodles now. They are wheat noodles with a firm and chewy texture. The texture is very important because the noodles are in hot soup while eating and might absorb too much soup and become too soft. It is very hard to find good noodles outside Japan. But you can use fresh angel hair pasta, which you can find in the refrigerated section at various supermarkets. The key is to boil the noodles in water with baking soda because that gives noodles a distinct Ramen noodle flavour.

    The other half of Ramen is the soup.

Ingredients

Salted pork
- 1 lb pork
- 1 teaspoon salt

Soup
- 6 cups water (1.5L)
- 50g ginger root, sliced
- 3 cloves garlic, skinned
- 1 bunch green onions
- 4 tablespoons soy sauce
- 2 tablespoons sake
- 1 teaspoon salt
- 1 teaspoon sesame oil

Noodles
- 9 oz fresh angel hair pasta (225g)
- 8 cups water (2L)
- 2 tablespoons baking soda

Topping
- Boiled egg halves
- Bean sprouts, blanched briefly
- Green onions, cut finely

Method

1. Rub salt on pork and let it sit overnight in the fridge.
2. In a pot, put water, ginger root, garlic, green onions and salted pork, and boil at high heat. Skim fat and other floating scums. Then cover, reduce to low heat, and simmer for 1½-2 hours. Let the broth and pork cool completely in pot.
3. Strain and save pork. Slice pork and set aside for a topping.
4. Prepare the rest of the toppings now as well (boiled eggs, blanched bean sprouts, cut green onions). before making the soup and noodles. Once the noodles are cooked, add the soup and toppings right away or the noodles will become soft.
5. Boil the broth and add soy sauce, sake, salt and sesame oil.
6. Let it simmer at very low heat until noodles are ready.
7. In boiling water in a pot, add baking soda (be careful, it may boil over), then add the fresh angel hair pasta. Cook the pasta for 30 seconds, and strain.
8. Divide noodles into bowls and add soup onto noodles. Top with boiled eggs, bean sprouts, green onions and sliced pork.

Tempting Tomatoes

I have an admission to make: tomatoes are a fruit I've always eaten in salads or chopped in pasta dishes, but never really rated as a proper vegetable dish – perhaps because of the often tasteless tomatoes we get year-round from glasshouses in the Netherlands.

Gone are the days when Scotland's Clyde Valley was chock-a-block with glasshouses growing fruits bursting with flavour. Or so I vaguely remember with rosy-spectacled nostalgia. High heating costs and serious damage by inclement weather, plus those cheap imports from our Dutch cousins, put growers out of business, replaced by garden centres and acres of dilapidated structures. But this dish gives tomatoes some flavour so they can be called a true vegetable dish.

Ingredients

Years of feeding a family have made me leave recipe books on the shelf and experiment with quantities and ingredients. Once I've mastered a recipe then it becomes boring to make and eat unless I indulge in a bit of trial and error. But if I taste as I go, then the error potential is minimal.

- Four or five large tomatoes (those on the vine have more flavour)
- Two or three spring onions
- A handful of dried fruit (currants and sultanas or dried cranberries). These help add sweetness to often fairly tasteless fruits.
- Balsamic vinegar
- Olive oil
- Dried basil/fresh basil
- Salt and pepper

Method

1. Slice some tomatoes. For four adults I use four or five good-sized tomatoes. Grate some pepper over them and, if you want, a little salt.
2. Chop a few spring onions and add to tomatoes with some currants, sultanas or cranberries. These add sweetness to the tomatoes. I tend to use sultanas rather than currants, or you could opt for raisins or a dried fruit mixture. Whatever you fancy or have in the cupboard.
3. Dust lightly with dried basil if you have it.
4. Add a good slug of dark balsamic vinegar and drizzle well with olive oil.
5. If I'm feeling especially generous I might add some chopped caperberries (a recent addition to the larder) or some green or black olives. All contribute different flavours to the final dish.

And there you have the quickest and easiest of salads and a perfect accompaniment to pasta and many other dishes.

Lentil Salad

Lentils have always been a staple in Scotland. Never used in anything other than soup, though. Red lentil soup made with a ham bone from the butcher was a favourite of both my mother and grandmother. Good filling, warming, nutritious food with which to face the vicissitudes of the Scottish winter.

Decades later I discovered Green and Puy lentils as well as the black ones called Beluga lentils. All these make amazing salads and side dishes.

Lentils are the oldest pulse crop known, and among the earliest crops domesticated in the Old World. Lentils are actually the seeds of a plant. They are amongst the most versatile and nutritious foods available, low in fat, and contain no cholesterol, so great if counting calories – and few of us aren't!

Ingredients

- 250g lentils of choice –
  – my preference is Beluga or Puy lentils
- your choice of tomatoes, cucumber, carrot, pepper (red is always my favourite and the sweetness works well in this salad), spring onions, whatever is to hand.
- Lemon juice
- Olive oil
- Feta cheese (optional)
- Fresh herbs
- Seasoning

Alternatively –
- An onion, chopped
- 250g mushrooms
- Fresh herbs
- Seasoning

Both options of this dish go deliciously well with salmon.

Method

1. Wash the lentils and put in a pan with plenty water and cook for required length of time. Check the packet details as some take longer to cook than others. When ready drain and start the magic bit.

Nowadays you can buy packs of black Beluga lentils ready to use, so no need even for cooking or dirtying a pot. You merely squeeze from packet into a dish and admire your handiwork.

2. While the lentils are cooking coerce a family member or roll up your own sleeves and chop the vegetables.

3. Mix vegetables and drained lentils together and moisten with the squeezed lemon juice. Season and drizzle liberally with olive oil.

4. Add cubes of Feta or other cheese if desired.

5. To add the final touch that really elevates this to heavenly, find some fresh herbs and tear into salad.

Alternatively –

Sweat sliced onion and mushrooms and add to the lentils along with herbs, lemon juice, olive oil and seasoning.

Carrot Salad

Carrots are a vastly under-rated vegetable, too often in Scotland only eaten sliced in mince or stews, or chopped in soups, much the same way they are also used across Europe and beyond. We associate them with an orange colour, though purple, black, red, white, and yellow cultivars exist.

My grandfather used to grow carrots in his allotment and that's maybe where I developed a liking for eating them raw.

In Madeira we often had bowls of grated raw carrot on the buffet, and occasionally you'd get a sprinkling of it on a salad, but this recipe is a moist and more interesting version of grated raw carrot, made infinately easier with my electric grater. Also a whizz at grating cheese. I can recommend.

Ingredients

- 1 lb of carrots, grated
- 3-4 ozs raisins or sultanas or dried cranberries
- 4 tablespoons mayonnaise
- salt
- grated allspice
- 12oz tin pineapple chunks, drained (optional)

Serves 6

Method

1. Grate carrots. If you don't have an electric grater ask hubby or one of the kids to do it. If hubby does it when finished you'll find him quite amenable to investing in the electric grater for you.
2. Tip into a bowl and add the other ingredients, mixing well.
3. Serve with salads or a range of meats.

I don't usually bother with the pineapple as I don't often have tinned fruit. I have occasionally added, satsumas or grapes instead. You can experiment, but it's good with just the dried fruit.

Pa amb Tomàquet – Catalan Tomato Bread

My wife Susan and I visited Catalonia in April, searching for the fascinating wildlife of the region. But we did do more than just birdwatching. On our last full day in Spain we toured Barcelona and met members of the independence movement, who were camping out in the Place da la Catalunya, which could be described as Barcelona's equivalent of Trafalgar Square.

We were impressed by the friendliness of the Catalan people and their determination to end rule from Madrid.

Is it always true that people seeking greater control over their future share a friendliness and humility that is rarely found in the strong and powerful?

Ingredients

- day old pan de cristal, cut in half
- vine-ripened tomatoes
- extra virgin olive oil
- sea salt or a fine flake salt
- fresh garlic – large bulb variety of garlic, such as Spanish or Red garlic, not Elephant Garlic, which is very mild.

Pa amb tomàquet is a classic dish found all over Catalonia. It is simple to make and comprises tomato and garlic spread on a traditional Catalan bread called "pan de cristal". Ciabatta or mini baguettes make acceptable alternatives. It can be eaten at breakfast, part of a tapas meal or as a snack. Also great for the barbeque. The trick is finding the best ingredients.

Method

1. Toast the bread over open flame or grill.
2. Slice a clove of garlic in half and rub over the surface of the bread.
3. Slice one large or two cherry tomatoes* in half and rub liberally across the bread, shredding the pulp in the process, until the bread is saturated, or you just have the tomato skin remaining.
4. Drizzle generously with olive oil.
5. Season with salt.
6. Enjoy.

For a more substantial version, top the bread with sliced Iberico or Serrano ham or anchovy fillets.

*Supermarket tomatoes are not a patch on home grown. I grow "Gardeners' Delight", which are small, sweet and very tasty. Tomatoes on the vine are the best shop alternative. Of course, the olive oil should be best extra virgin.

29

Tasty Haggis Bites

Ingredients

As every Haggis lover knows, Burns night is not the only time to enjoy our favourite food. Haggis is now loved all over the world, in spite of the Americans once blowing one up on the runway in New York after the sniffer dogs showed great interest in a case containing one.

There is a belief that after a hunt the parts of the animal that wouldn't keep were chopped and stuffed into the stomach then boiled with ever-to-hand oatmeal, ensuring in a waste -not-want-not economy that food was not wasted.

Of course we all know a haggis is a small Scottish creature with legs longer on one side to enable it to run around steep Highland hills without falling over. According to a poll, 33% of American visitors to Scotland believed haggis is such an animal.

- Haggis
- 1 cup breadcrumbs and extra for coating balls
- Half a cup grated Parmesan cheese.
- Freshly ground black pepper.
- oil for deep-frying

Method

1. Mix well together the breadcrumbs, the parmesan and black pepper.
2. Using a large teaspoon, scoop up enough Haggis to form into balls about the size of small walnuts.
3. Coat well in the breadcrumb mix and drop into a hot oil till crispy. About 2 minutes.
4. Drain on kitchen paper and enjoy.

Onion Bhaji
The Classic Indian Starter with a twist

My passion for Indian food started early, when my family made rather poor quality curry using pre-mixed curry powder, often too old to have kept its flavour. No wonder many British people were put off curry.

I was lucky to be directed to "curry corner" in Birmingham, full of competing Indian restaurants and where a huge variety of dishes were available, from all over the sub-continent.

I went through flirtations with the hottest food, such as the infamous Bangalore Phal, showing off to my friends, but I also learnt that Indian food was much more than scorching chili heat.

Scottish links with India date from the foray of many there after the failure of the Company of Scotland and the Scottish imperial adventure at Darien in the late 1690s.

Ingredients

- 2 large onions, finely sliced
- 75g plain flour
- 1 tablespoon cornflour
- 1 teaspoon ground coriander seeds
- 1 teaspoon ground cumin seeds
- 1 teaspoon honey (optional)
- 150ml cold water, or 100ml water and 1 large egg
- vegetable or sunflower oil for frying

This recipe uses a mixture of cornflour and plain flour, instead of the more traditional garam (chickpea) flour. In my view, it works well. Using an egg instead of some of the water adds a richness to the result. Happy eating.

Method

1. Mix the plain flour, cornflour and spices in a bowl.
2. Add in the water (or beaten egg and water mixture) and stir to form a smooth batter.
3. Drop in the slices of onion and stir until the onion is fully coated.
5. Heat ½ inch of oil in a pan until smoking hot, then drop in spoonfuls of the battered onion.
6. If the bhajis are a little thick, pat them out so they are just a little deeper than the frying oil.
7. Once the bottom has browned, flip and cook the other side.
8. Remove onto kitchen paper to absorb excess oil and serve.

This amount should make a generous portion for two or, if made smaller, sufficient for four.

Rick's Sandwich ...and more

In 1975 during the early days of self-employment my family needed an income, so Liz, my wife, took on an early morning job so it was my duty to make up the twins' lunch box. As well as the usual sandwich fillings of ham, cheese, tomato and lettuce, I occasionally filled some with currants or sultanas – which may seem a bit off-beat but I love them myself.

Becoming aware of my eccentric food combinations the twins would open their lunch boxes with a glance at each other which said, 'What the heck has Dad inflicted on us today?'

They survived and are now healthy 50 year olds – I credit the currants!

Raisins and sultanas are produced from the same grape, the difference being the way they are dried. Currants are also made from small grapes.

Ingredients

- two slices of bread; my choice is wholemeal cut from an unsliced loaf.
2. butter or spread.
3. currants or sultanas; and why not stoned dates or prunes.
4. thin slices of Cheddar for additional zing.

Years of watching Liz effortlessly produce tasty meals from whatever ingredients were in the cupboards, emboldened me to be more adventurous with food combinations.

One of my own favourites is to boil a pan of tatties and mash in a tin of pilchards in tomato sauce. Result – a simple but tasty dinner one day and fried fishcakes for breakfast the next.

Liz won't even touch this!

Method

Come on – who can't make a sandwich!

Nanbanzuke

Nanbanzuke is marinated and deep-fried fish in vinegar sauce with vegetables. The vinegar in the sauce gives a refreshing flavour. Nanbanzuke is more home-cooking than restaurant food, so is not often found at UK Japanese restaurants.

"Nanban" means "foreign," indicating Portugal and Spain, from a period in the 17th century when Japan traded with these countries. During this period, new cooking methods such as deep-frying, and ingredients like hot pepper and onions were introduced to Japan. "Zuke" (or "dzuke") means marinated.

Japan is proud of its Scottish links, with Thomas Blake Glover becoming very influential in Japan after his arrival in 1859, forging trading links with Scottish companies and becoming pivotal in the growth of Mitsubishi as an international conglomerate.

Ingredients

- 2 saba (mackerel) fillets
- salt
- 2 tablespoons katakuriko (potato starch) or flour
- ½ medium onion
- 2 inch medium carrot
- 2 green onions
- ½ cup rice vinegar
- ½ cup dashi
- 1 tablespoon sugar
- 2 tablespoons soy sauce
- 2 tablespoons mirin
- 1 tablespoon sake
- 1-2 chili pods
- Oil for deep-frying

Servings 3-4

Mackerel is typically used, but salmon is also good. Fish pieces are coated with flour before deep-frying so the fish absorbs sauce.

Method

1. Liberally sprinkle salt over fish, and leave for 15 minutes.
2. Remove any moisture from the fish with a paper towel.
3. Cut fillets into 5-6 pieces each and coat lightly in katakuriko.
4. Slice onion very thinly.
5. Cut carrot into thin matchsticks.
6. Slice green onions thinly and diagonally.
7. Put all the vegetables together in a glass dish or other heat-proof medium-deep container.
8. In a pot, mix rice vinegar, dashi, sugar, soy sauce, mirin, sake, and chili pods.
9. Cook to a boil and remove from heat.
10. Pour the hot sauce over vegetables.
11. Deep fry the fish at 350ºF (180ºC) for 3-5 minutes.
12. Remove and immediately add to the vinegar sauce, and coat with the sauce.

Serve with thinly sliced onions, carrots, green or red peppers, or pieces of kabocha pumpkin or eggplants.

37

Swedish Marinated Herring

Ingredients

I was never fond of fish, and herrings, kippers really turned me off. My husband likes herrings cooked in oatmeal and I can't bear to be in the kitchen when he cooks them. The smell! Ugh!

Years ago, when you could sail DFDS from Newcastle to Esbjerg in Denmark or Gothenburg in Sweden we used to throw the kids in the car and go off on holiday. That's where I got a taste for marinated herring. Afterwards, we used to buy jars in Ikea, but preparing your own is so much better.

Herring for years was a staple Scottish dish, caught all round our shores and exported around the world. Anyone who hasn't read Neil Gunn's *The Silver Darlings* has missed out on a treat. And Gunn's silver darlings are celebrated too every year in Eyemouth's Herring Queen festival.

- ¼ cup salt
- 5 cups water
- 1 pound herring fillets
- 2 cups white balsamic or white wine vinegar
- ¼ cup sugar
- 1 teaspoon whole mustard seed
- 2 teaspoons whole allspice
- 2 teaspoons black peppercorns
- 3 bay leaves
- a few juniper berries (I like lots as I love their flavour)
- 1 lemon, thinly sliced
- 1 medium red onion thinly sliced

Serve with Scandinavian, German or Polish rye bread, some cheese and salad. Yummy.

Method

1. Heat 4 cups of water sufficiently to dissolve the salt.
2. Allow this brine to cool to room temperature.
3. Submerge the herring fillets in the brine and refrigerate overnight, or up to 24 hours. This brining extracts extra moisture from the fish and keeps them firm. Otherwise the herring can become mushy.
4. When herrings are brined, drain off liquid.
5. Bring the sugar, vinegar, remaining cup of water, juniper berries and spices to the boil.
5. Simmer for 5 minutes, then turn off the heat and allow the marinade to infuse as it cools.
6. Layer the herrings in a glass jar with the sliced lemon and red onion.
7. Pour over the cooled pickling liquid and seal the jars.
8. Wait at least a day before eating.
9. These should store in the fridge for up to 1 month.

Mackerel Pâté

Oily fish are high in long-chain omega-3 fatty acids, which may help prevent heart disease, and are an important source of vitamin D, particularly important in dark northern winters. Sunlight is another major source of vitamin D. Salmon, mackerel, sardines, trout and herring are all examples of oily fish.

Mackerel pâté is an excellent choice for a healthy and nourishing fish dish especially for those less keen on oily fish.

The supplement capsules market is a billion dollar industry. Liver oil capsules are popular but are a very different product in that they contain high levels of vitamin A.

Far better to eat interesting food with balanced nutritional and vitamin values.

Traditional mackerel pâté recipes used cream. Yogurt is a healthier option, leaving a less cloying and more pleasing taste. Use Greek or Turkish plain yogurt for best results.

Ingredients

- around 200g of cooked mackerel
- 120g of soft butter
- 4 heaped tablespoons of plain Greek yogurt (3 of a thinner yogurt)
- ½ lemon or whole lime
- sea salt and black pepper
- a mix of dried herbs or chopped fresh herbs as available

Alternatively:
Kipper pate
- 2 poach in the bag skinned cooked kippers instead of mackerel

Sardine Pate:
- 1 can of sardines

Method

1. Skin the cooked mackerel and place in food processor with the zest of half a lemon or whole lime and the juice and blitz till well crumbled.
2. Add other ingredients and blitz again till smooth.
3. Spoon into small dishes and place in fridge to chill and firm.
4. Serve on bread or toast with salad.

Kipper pate
1. Follow above method using 2 cooled poach in the bag skinned cooked kippers. Adjust butter and yogurt to compensate for kipper juices.

Sardine Pate:
Drain a can of sardines and follow above method reducing butter and yogurt in proportion to the weight of sardines.

Finnan Haddock and Poached Egg

This is my grandmother's recipe. She lived in St Andrews and in the winter she took in students with full board. Finan Haddock and Poached Egg was a regular meal offered to the students for tea.

In the beginning she had only male students but they broke so many chairs by swinging back on them as they supposedly studied that Gran decided on only female students after that. The broken chairs never got mended and were found many years later stacked in the attic!

I preferred when the girl students stayed as they would let me wear their traditional red gowns which were worn on the shoulder for first year students then gradually more and more off the shoulders as the years went by.

Ingredients

- 800g undyed smoked finnan haddock
- 250ml milk
- ground black or cayenne pepper
- 4 large eggs
- 1 tablespoon vinegar

Serves 4

Finnan haddock is cold-smoked haddock, a method of smoking with green wood and peat in north-east Scotland.

Method

1. Cut fish into portion sizes.
2. Heat frying pan over a medium heat and add fish.
3. Pour over milk or cream.
4. Bring up to slow simmer and cover with a lid or large plate.
5. Turn off the heat. Leave the flavours to infuse and the fish to continue cooking in the latent heat for 5 minutes. The fish should have changed to a milky-opaque all the way through.
6. Put a pan of water on a medium heat and bring to the boil.
7. Add vinegar.
8. Drop in eggs gently and simmer for 2-3 minutes till the whites are firm but the yolks stll soft. Test by removing an egg in a skimming ladle and gently pressing the yolk.
9. Remove and drain.
10. Put the fish on heated deep soup plates.
11. Boil up the cooking liquid and reduce slightly, taste and season. Place eggs on top of the fish. Pour over the milk or cream.
Serve with bread and butter and a pot of tea.

Fettunta

When I was an extremely poor student and single parent of two young children I had to be extremely inventive on how to make meals which were cheap, nourishing and appealing. I didn't always succeed but I have one recipe which I am still asked for today and my son is 48.

Quite often at the end of the week I would have to create something out of the remains of the fridge, et, voilà, Fettunta was born. (I always found that making up a name for a creation gave it instant appeal and gravitas.)

Scots became aware of the potato in the second half of the 17th century. Although tatties are regarded as a traditional vegetable initially there was great reluctance to grow and to eat them, But their ability to survive in stony ground and a damp climate changed this to reliance.

Ingredients

The amounts of each depend entirely on the contents of the fridge but let's say the the following:
- 2 lbs potatoes
- 2-3 cloves garlic
- 2-3 ozs butter
- 2 large eggs
- 4 ozs cheese

The Yes Brittany Group are in residence.

Method

1. Boil and then drain and mash potatoes with the butter and mashed garlic.
2. Mix it well with a wooden spoon as it helps to smooth it into deliciousness.
3. Add some seasoning.
4. Add two eggs whisked.
5. Keep pounding away with the wooden spoon and then add cheese.
6. When thoroughly mixed place in ovenproof bowl and bake at 180ºC for about 25-30 minutes.
7. Serve with a tomato and red onion salad and home made vinaigrette.
8. More cheese is always welcome.

Red Dragon Pie

This is a great family dish. It's a good way to get children to eat beans, grains and vegetables as it's so similar to Shepherd's Pie.

The Chinese call aduki beans 'red dragon' or 'red wonder' beans as they have found them to be so full of goodness. The cooking liquid from the aduki beans is thought by some to be a tonic for the kidneys.

Tell the children they will have the power of the dragon after eating this!

The tea trade, for which Clyde shipyards built fast clipper vessels, and the opium trade saw Scots merchants dominant in the China Trade and trade with the East Indies, with Scots' affinity with the Chinese fuelling a fascination for all things oriental and in particular Canton silver.

Ingredients

- 110g aduki beans
- 50g wheat grain or rice
- 2 pints water for soaking
- 2 pints water for boiling
- 1 tablespoon of oil
- 1 onion, peeled and finely chopped
- 225g carrots, scrubbed and diced
- 1-2 tablespoons soy sauce
- 2 tablespoons tomato puree
- 1 teaspoon mixed herbs
- ½ pint aduki bean stock
- salt and freshly ground pepper
- 450g potatoes peeled
- 25g butter

Serves 4

Method

1. Pre-heat the oven to gas mark 4, 350ºF, 180ºC
2. Wash the aduki beans and the wheat grain or rice and soak them overnight or steep them in boiling water for 1 hour.
3. Drain and rinse, then bring them to the boil in fresh water and cook for 50 minutes or until the wheat grain or rice is fairly soft. Drain, reserving the stock.
4. Heat the oil in a saucepan and fry the onion for 5 minutes.
5. Add the carrots and cook for 2-3 minutes.
6. Add the cooked beans and grains.
7. Mix the soy sauce, tomato puree and herbs with the stock and pour this over the bean and vegetable mixture.
8. Bring to the boil and simmer for 20-30 minutes, so that the flavours are well blended.
9. Season to taste. Add a little more liquid if necessary so that the final mixture is moist. Transfer into a greased casserole.
10. Boil the potatoes until soft and mash with butter. Season well. Spread the mashed potato over the beans and vegetables.
11. Bake for 35-40 minutes until potato is crisp and brown.

Dundee/Calcutta Beef Curry

My parents spent 3 years or so in Calcutta 1948 – 51ish. My dad worked as a mill mechanic in the jute industry. Many Dundee families did the trip - it was good money and a way of getting ahead post-war when times were hard.

My granny was a jute mill worker in Dundee. It goes back a long way. My mother learned how to cook this traditional hot beef curry. I was brought up on it - first just a beef stew with rice and lentils then as I got older I'd get more and more of the hot curry sauce. This version is the closest I've managed to get but still not quite the real thing.

It is said to be impossible to ignore the legacy of the Scots in Calcutta (now Kolkata) and Bengal where they were influential in shaping the fortunes of the city.

Ingredients

Serves 4 pretty generously - it's filling!
- 700g of stewing beef cut into chunks
- 1 large or two smaller onions sliced
- 2 large or 3 smaller cooking apples, peeled, cored and roughly chopped
- 50g of butter for frying. I use ghee but assume mum used butter
- 3 heaped dessert spoons of curry powder. Mum used Madras I think. I tend to go for medium but up to you. I add extra turmeric. It should be yellow!
- 150g – 200g sultanas
- 200g red lentils
- 300g white rice

Method

1. In large frying pan, fry the onions and brown the beef with the curry powder.
2. Add the apples. The smell really takes me back.
3. Once meat is browned and onions softened add about half a litre of water and the sultanas.
4. Simmer over low hear until the meat is tender, the apples are pretty much collapsing and the sultanas are plump and swollen - about 45 minutes. You might need to add a bit extra water. That's it really.
5. Make a simple lentil Dahl and plain boiled rice.
6. Serve rice first, then beef curry sauce on top, finish with good dollop of lentils.

   I knew one girl at school with a similar family history who would put sliced banana or dessicated coconut on top but my parents frowned upon that so I've never tried it.

My older brother was born in Calcutta in 1949. Above is his christening photo. Mum and dad are the the rather glamorous couple in centre. Brother is being held aloft by his godmother.

Scottish Pizza

In those far-off days of the past, before Pizza joints were found on every hight street and on every corner, Italian restaurants were where you went to celebrate, if your finances could stretch to it. As far as many of us were concerned, before we became cosmopolitanised by cheap foreign holidays in the sun, Italy meant only two foods – pizza and pasta. Now pasta seemed a bit too much like our own macaroni and cheese, so pizza it had to be.

Before the introduction of breadmakers, making a yeasted base for pizza required some forethought and planning, but a pizza was still regarded as a welcome change from the usual mince and tatties. So my mother and I used to make this version with a scone-like base. A Scottish variation on the Italian.

Ingredients

- 1lb self-raising flour
- 3 teaspoons baking powder
- 8 tablespoons oil
- ½ pint of milk
- 1 tin chopped tomatoes (drained) or sliced fresh tomatoes
- cooked bacon or salami, diced
- garlic, crushed
- 8 ozs cheese grated (in those days I used cheddar)
- salt and pepper
- dried or fresh herbs (basil or origano)
- paprika (optional but wonderful)

You can use less cheese but we're cheese fanatics so like plenty.

Makes six good servings.

We eventually made it to Italy

Method

1. Mix flour, salt and pepper, baking powder.
2. Add oil and milk.
3. Mix to a dough and spread into an oiled swiss roll tin.
4. Crush garlic and spread over dough.
5. Cover with tomatoes and diced cooked bacon or salami.
6. Sprinkle with herbs.
7. Top with cheese.
8. Sprinkle with paprika.
9. Bake in oven at 425ºF for about 25-30 minutees until cheese is sizzling and base is cooked.
10. Cut into servings.

Stovies

Ma Granny made stovies every Hogmanay and Ne'erday for family parties. Ma Uncle Tony would play the box and all my Uncles would do a turn. Uncle Bobby would sing Scottish Soldier, Uncle Eddie singing Hello Dolly and Northern Lights of Auld Aberdeen and my Dad would fall asleep all fuelled by bottles of whisky.

The Wummin would drink Advocaat, make sandwiches and tell husbands they had had enough to drink.

The stovies would appear, with miracle-like rejuvenation effects on all, and with renewed energy the party would go on for a couple of days.

Stovies on the stove for all who came first footin as long as they did a turn.

The name stovies originates from the French étuvée meaning braised – a reminder of the Auld Alliance.

Ingredients

- 3 lb tatties
- 1 large onion
- 1 lb mince/lamb/corned beef/vegie stuff if really required
- 2 oz beef dripping or lard or oil
- half pint water/meat stock/veg
- salt/season to taste

Serves 6 maybe.

Editor's note: We like ours dredged with good pinhead oatmeal.

Method

1. Chop onion into pot, add fat and gently cook for 5 minutes.
2. Add meat. Stir into onion and cook until light brown.
3. Peel tatties and hurtle intae pot.
4. Chuck in water, stock, salt etc.
5. Bring to boil and simmer for 30 minutes until tatties are soft, shoggle pot at times.
6. Have a nip while waiting.
7. If it burns at bottom, dinnae fash, tastes better.
8. Serve with oat cakes/crusty bread/lots of whisky.

Brie, Artichoke and Tomato Pie

Ingredients

My husband joined me in becoming vegetarian about a year ago and I am forever hunting tasty recipes which satisfy him as much as meat. This recipe fulfils this. It is a deliciously rich dish which meat eaters love. I recently cooked it for a large dinner party and had to bake two pies to feed everyone. When I brought the second one to the table one guest said, 'Blimey, is it one each!'. Luckily this was a joke.

The meal was enjoyed by all and I was asked for the recipe by more than one guest. (The dish is high in fat and therefore not suitable for enjoying too often.)

Brie is a soft cow's-milk cheese named after the French region where it originated. Bries are now also made in Scotland though most of our traditional cheeses have now disappeared.

- 1 puff pastry sheet, defrosted
- 8 oz wheel of Brie cheese
- 4 ozs canned artichoke hearts
- 4 ozs sundried tomatoes
- 2 ozs pesto (about half a small jar)

Notes: When I make this for just two people, I use a smaller cheese as shown in the photo.

I have also made this with shortcrust Pastry and it was still tasty but the Puff Pastry gives a more luxurious feel.

Method

1. Preheat oven to 180ºF or gas mark 4.
2. Lightly grease a baking sheet and roll out the pastry sheet onto it.
3. Place the Brie in the centre of the pastry.
4. Chop the artichokes and sundried tomatoes and place in bowl. Add Pesto and mix.
5. Spoon this mixture over the top of the cheese.
6. Fold the pastry up and over the top of the cheese and topping and pinch at seams. It should look rustic.
7. Bake in the preheated oven for 30 minutes.
8. Serve with salad or cooked vegetables of your choice.

Kefta Middle Eastern Spiced Meatballs

Spiced meatballs are common in one form or another from Morocco in the west through the Middle East (kefta or kufta), to Greece (keftedes), Turkey (köfte), Armenia (kufta), Iran (kufteh, or koofteh) and all the way to India (kofta) in the east. All names for these little balls of wonder derive from the Persian verb kuftan, which means "to grind." And all are delicious. (And not so different from our own mince patties.)

Called tzatziki in Greece, the cooling combination of yoghurt and cucumber is popular all around the eastern Mediterranean. The Turkish version is called cacik. In Iran, it is known as mast-o-khiyar. Bulgarians call it tarator. For Iraqis, it is jajeek.
  Ttzatziki goes great with gyros sandwiches or keftedes meatballs.

Ingredients

- 2 lbs ground lamb or beef, or a mixture of the two
- 1 onion, minced
- ½ bunch fresh parsley or mint, finely chopped
- 1 tablespoon ground cumin
- 2 teaspoons cinnamon
- 1 teaspoon Allspice (optional)
- salt and pepper to season
- ¼ cup of oil
Makes about 20 meatballs

Tzatziki
- 1 cucumber, peeled, seeded and grated
- 1 teaspoon salt
- 2 cups thick, Greek-style yoghurt
- juice of ½ a lemon
- 1 or 2 cloves garlic, minced
- ¼ cup olive oil
Makes about 2½ cups

Method

1. Place the ground beef or lamb, onion, herbs, spices, salt and pepper in a large bowl and knead together well. Wrap in plastic and chill for 1 to 2 hours to allow the flavours to mingle and make the meat easier to handle.
2. Form the meat mixture into balls, patties or ovals the size of a small egg.
3. Heat the oil in a skillet over medium flame and, working in batches, sauté the meatballs until browned on all sides and cooked through. Browned meatballs can also be finished in a 350ºF oven.
4. Serve as is or in pita bread as a sandwich with tzatziki sauce. It's also excellent served with rice or couscous.

Tzatziki
1. In large bowl, toss the cucumber with the salt and set aside for 5-10 minutes. Squeeze cucumber to get rid of excess moisture.
2. Add remaining ingredients and stir together until blended.
3. Adjust seasoning. Serve well chilled as an appetizer with bread or pita, or as sauce for souvlaki, gyros or roasted meats.

Moroccan Vegetable & Honey Tagine

I first tried this recipe when a friend returned from a trip to Morocco (see photo) and kindly presented me with a jar of Ras el Hanout which was entirely new to me. (I have since found it in most supermarkets and buy it regularly.) My friend organised a Moroccan evening for his friends and asked us each to bring a Moroccan dish to share. I couldn't refuse the challenge so went for a traditional Tagine which is a rich spicy stew with intense flavours. It often features lamb but this is a vegetarian/vegan version which turns humble chickpeas into a delicious feast as they absorb the gorgeous sweet and spicy flavours. It goes well with couscous and looks lovely finished with a dollop of natural yoghurt and perhaps some fresh coriander leaves.

Ingredients

- 1 teaspoon sunflower oil
- 3 cloves of garlic, peeled and finely chopped
- 2 tablespoons Ras el Hanout paste (or 1 teaspoon cumin seeds, 2 teaspoons ground cinnamon, 2 teaspoons paprika and finely grated 2.5 cm piece of fresh ginger)
- 2 teaspoons tomato puree
- 400g can chopped tomatoes
- 400g can chickpeas, drained and rinsed
- 3 red peppers, deseeded and chopped into 2 cm pieces
- 2 large courgettes, cut into 1 cm thick slices
- handful of sultanas (if liked)
- 2 teaspoons honey (use agave syrup if Vegan)
- 200ml hot vegetable stock
- 4 teaspoons lemon juice
- salt and pepper

Method

1. Heat the oil in a large saucepan over a medium heat.
2. Add garlic (and fresh ginger if using) and cook for a few minutes until softened and aromatic.
3. Add Ras el Hanout (or separate spices if using) and cook for a minute or so stirring constantly
4. Add tomato puree, chopped tomatoes, chickpeas, red peppers, courgettes and sultanas and stir together to combine
5. Add the vegetable stock and honey (or agave syrup) and allow to simmer for about 30 minutes, stirring every 5 minutes.
6. Check the vegetables are tender. If not cook for a further 10 minutes and check again.
7. When cooked finish with lemon juice and salt and pepper to taste.

This dish has turned into a family favourite, especially on cold winter evenings and brings memories of our friend who sadly died last year.

Leftover Welsh Lamb Shepherd's Pie

A Welsh Slow-roast lamb is a delight to have at dinner but can lead to a loss of leftovers plan, but the lamb leftovers can be made even better if you make this Welsh shepherd's pie dish.

Our Celtic cousins in Wales may claim the best lamb but I'm certain that would be challenged in Scotland where Scotch Lamb is one of the fourteen Scottish products protected by one of the EU protection schemes for quality regional food products – a protection which is likely to be lost when we leave the EU at the end of March 2019.

Ingredients

- 1 tablespoon olive oil
- 1 large onion, chopped
- 2 carrots, chopped
- 2 celery sticks, chopped
- 3 garlic cloves, chopped
- 1 tablespoon fresh thyme
- 75ml red wine
- 500g leftover slow-roast lamb, shredded
- 100ml lamb or chicken stock
- 2 tablespoons Worcestershire sauce
- 3 tablespoons tomato ketchup
- 1 tablespoon tomato purée
- 800g floury potatoes, cubed
- 3 tablespoons butter
- 2 large free-range egg yolks
- 25g grated parmesan, plus extra for sprinkling

Serves 6

Method

1. Heat the oven to 200°C/fan180°C/gas 6.
2. Heat olive oil in a large frying pan, then gently cook onion, carrots, celery and garlic for 10-12 minutes until tender.
3. Add the thyme and red wine, then simmer for 2-3 minutes.
4. Add the leftover lamb, stock, Worcestershire sauce, ketchup and tomato purée, then season.
5. Simmer gently for 15 minutes until mixture has reduced.
6. Put the potatoes in a large pan of cold salted water, bring to boil, simmer for 12 minutes or until tender. Drain, return the potatoes to the pan and mash until smooth. Beat in butter and egg yolks, then stir through the grated parmesan.
7. Spread lamb mixture in a 1.5-litre ovenproof dish and top with the mash. Sprinkle over a little extra parmesan and season.
8. Bake in the oven for 20-25 minutes until golden on top and bubbling.

One Pan Caribbean Jerk Chicken

The fusion of Asian stir-fry and fiery Caribbean seasoning makes a wonderful sweet and spicy dish.

Served over hot white rice it will give you the taste and experience of Jamaica.

And don't forget a glass or two of good dark Rum.

The Scottish-Caribbean link is centuries old, but grew rapidly from the early 18th century with the slave trade – not one of Scotland's finest periods. By the late 18th century, Britain dominated the West Indies and along with other European countries transported black African slaves to work the plantations of the Caribbean. Scottish slave masters and slave owners played a significant role in slavery, with Jamaica becoming a large producer of sugar, coffee, rum and spices, transported by ship to Greenock, Port Glasgow and Leith.

Ingredients

- 1 tablespoon vegetable oil
- 1 green pepper, seeded and cubed
- 1 red pepper, seeded and cubed
- 4 tablespoons sliced onion
- 350g skinless, boneless chicken breast, cut into strips
- 2½ teaspoons Caribbean jerk seasoning
- 125ml plum sauce
- 1 tablespoon soy sauce
- 4 tablespoons chopped roasted peanuts

Serves 2

Method

1. Heat the oil in a large frying pan over medium-high heat.
2. Cook and stir the peppers and onion in the oil until slightly tender, 5 to 7 minutes.
3. Remove peppers and onion from the pan and set aside.
4. Add the chicken to the pan; season with jerk seasoning.
5. Cook and stir chicken until no longer pink inside.
6. Pour the plum sauce in with the chicken.
7. Add the peppers and onions; toss to combine.
8. Cook until the peppers and onions are heated completely, 3 to 5 minutes.
9. Sprinkle with soy sauce and chopped peanuts to serve.

Hungarian Gulasch

I had a rather parochial upbringing in Buckinghamshire in the 1970-80s: never ate garlic or other funny foreign fare, never went abroad, hated French lessons. Mid-1990s I got into Scottish dancing and met this lovely lass with a Scottish accent. When asked which part of Scotland she came from she laughed because she comes from a very rural part of former East Germany. She was in Edinburgh as a student. Hungarian Goulash was the first meal she ever cooked for me, the first time I'd ever had sauerkraut or even paprika and caraway. Even diced pork (rather than beef) was unusual for me.

Looking back 22 years later, I see that 'exotic' meal as a turning point in my life, one of real enrichment. We are now married with four bi-lingual kids: multicultural food being a big part of our life.

Ingredients

This warming winter dish from Szeged in southern Hungary is widely cooked in Germany and is a firm family favourite:

Gulasch

- 600g diced pork
- 250g diced onions
- 2 crushed cloves of garlic
- 2 tablespoons paprika powder
- 500g mild sauerkraut
- a sprinkling of caraway seeds
- 125 ml soured cream

This is best served with some proper bread or potato dumplings:

Potato Dumplings

- 1 kg potatoes, cooked, cooled and then minced
- 1 cup (250ml) potato starch
- 1 egg
- pinch of salt

Method

Gulasch

1. Brown the meat in a lidded casserole, add the onions and cook until soft.
2. Add the garlic and paprika powder.
3. Fluff up the sauerkraut and place it on top of the meat, sprinkling it with caraway seeds.
4. Put the lid on and cook on a low heat for 40-50 mins, stirring the whole dish half way through the cooking time.
5. Stir in the soured cream just before serving.

Potato Dumplings

6. Combine the ingredients in a large bowl.
7. Knead until well combined.
8. Form small dumplings about 2 inches in diameter.
9. Put into boiling water, turn the heat right down to simmering point.
10. After 15 mins they should be cooked, rising to the surface of the water. Take out with a slotted spoon.

Creamy Mushroom Risotto

My liking for risotto comes not so much from Italy as from an Italian restaurant in Melrose.

This is one of those dishes that fits the bill when you can't think what to have for dinner.

My mother used to say on such days that she wished someone would invent a new animal, and I often know how she felt.

This is my version of risotto and if any irate Italian wants to take me to task, then in my defence I'll just say that dishes are rarely static, they evolve to suit what's in the fridge and cupboard, how much time you have, and what you feel like doing. If creativity is the order of the day then you might experiment. Nothing wrong with that. The proof is in the eating. If plates are empty then pat yourself on the back.

Ingredients

- 500g Arborio rice
- 2 onions
- 250g mushrooms* (I like the chestnut mushrooms as they have more flavour)
- 8ozs Pecorino cheese, grated
- cream
- olive oil
- chicken stock cube
- salt and pepper

The risotto can also be made with dried mushrooms, in which case reduce the quantity, or a mixture of fresh and dried.

Makes 4-6 helpings, depending how hungry folk are.

Method

1. Slice onions and mushrooms and sweat till softened in oil in a pan. I find a large shallow pan best for this.
2. Add a little salt (not too much as cheese is salty) and pepper along with some dried mixed herbs.
3. Add the rice and stir so that grains absorb flavour.
4. Add water (about a pint but you may need a little more).
5. Crumble in stock cube.
6. Bring to boil then simmer, stirring occasionally, and adding more water if necessary, until rice is softened.
7. Stir in grated cheese.
8. Add sufficient cream to loosen consistency.
9. Adjust seasoning, adding more salt if required.
10. Serve with Tempting Tomato salad or a green salad with a French dressing.

Viking Pizza

All the taste of the Mediterranean, drawing on it's Italian heritage but making it a feast for Northern Viking descendants to celebrate the richness of a heritage gratefully plundered from our Southern European neighbours, but with none of the thin coating of toppings associated with a less endowed baking so common in modern price-conscious commercial products.

This is an all-in pizza, rich, filling, plundered and fit for an army of independistas on a peaceful march to become an independent European state again. By taking from others and making it something of our own we follow a great European tradition, saluting as we borrow in friendship and solidarity.

Ingredients

Base
- 600g white bread flour
- 100g wholemeal
- 1 teaspoon each of yeast, salt and sugar
- generous splash of olive oil
- mixed herbs or fenugreek
- around half a litre water.

Topping for Viking Pizza
- 1 tablespoon each of pesto and passata
- 2 large onions, sliced
- 2 stalks of celery
- 1 large red pepper
- 3 or 4 cloves of garlic diced
- 3 sliced gherkins
- 4 sliced sundried tomatoes
- 150g of mushrooms, sliced
- 5 tomatoes sliced
- 150g sliced salami
- 500g sliced gouda or cheddar
- paprika

Serves 8-12 Viking appetites

Method

1. Smear the pizza tray with oil.
2. Use a breadmaker on the dough setting or mix in a bowl following the bread recipe on page 95.
3. Stretch and pull the dough to cover beyond the edges until the tray is covered and the overlap is on your worktop.
4. Mix 1 tablespoon each of pesto and passata in a small bowl.
5. Smear the base with the pesto passata mix.
6. Add the sliced ingredients more or less in the order given in ingredients column.
7. Cover with cheese slices in double layer.
8. Fold in overlapping edges to form crust.
9. Dust top liberally with paprika.
10. Bake for 35 minutes at 200ºC.
11. Serve with a bowl of olives adding a splash of olive oil, juice of half a lemon or lime and mixed dried herbs - mix and top with a few fresh basil leaves.

Chicken Enchiladas

This delicious recipe is a quick and easy meal that is perfect for a quick supper or fun child-friendly party food that will add a little bit of Mexican magic to your dinner table.

Links between Scotland and Mexico appear to go back a long way with the St Andrew's Society of Mexico more than 120 years old, one of the oldest associations in Mexico.

Edinburgh born Frances "Fanny" Erskine Inglis, later the Marquesa of Calderón de la Barca, was a 19th-century, woman of letters, traveler, companion to the royal family of Spain, and travel writer best known for her 1843 book *Life in Mexico*, widely regarded as one of the most influential Latin American travel narratives of the 19th century.

Ingredients

- 4 skinless, boneless chicken breast fillets
- 1 onion, chopped
- 225ml soured cream
- 125g grated Cheddar cheese
- 1 tablespoon dried parsley
- ½ teaspoon dried oregano
- ½ teaspoon ground black pepper
- ½ teaspoon salt (optional)
- 400g passata
- 125ml water
- 1 tablespoon chilli powder
- 5 tablespoons chopped green pepper
- 1 clove garlic, minced
- 8 flour tortillas
- 300g salsa or enchilada sauce
- 85g grated Cheddar cheese

Serves 8

Method

1. Preheat oven to 180º C / Gas 4.
2. In a medium, non-stick frying pan over medium heat, cook chicken until no longer pink and juices run clear.
3. Drain excess fat.
4. Cube the chicken and return it to the pan.
5. Add the onion, soured cream, 125g Cheddar cheese, parsley, oregano and ground black pepper.
6. Heat until cheese melts.
7. Stir in salt, passata, water, chilli powder, green pepper and garlic.
8. Roll even amounts of the mixture in the tortillas.
Arrange in a 22x33cm/9x13 inch baking dish.
9. Cover with salsa or enchilada sauce and sprinkle with 85g Cheddar cheese.
10. Bake uncovered in the preheated oven for 20 minutes.
11. Cool 10 minutes before serving.

Leftover Chicken Nachos

Nachos are quick and easy comfort food which can be made using various types of fillings.

If like me you have chicken leftovers from your Sunday roast then this is a ridiculously easy supper that is great for using up leftover chicken in no time at all. Your kids will love it, though you may want to leave the jalapeno chillies off theirs.

The Scottish and Welsh left their mark in Mexico, especially in the states of Hidalgo, Jalisco, Aguascalientes, and Veracruz. More recently, after visiting his parents in Mexico, an Aberdeen entrepreneur found a way to inject some Scottish flavour into Tequila, Mexico's most famous export, by aging it in whisky casks from Speyside. He thought it would be cool to put both national drinks together.

Ingredients

- 1-2 packets tortilla chips
- 3-4 shallots, chopped
- 1 pepper, diced
- 4 tomatoes, diced
- leftover roast chicken, diced
- jalapeño slices to taste
- 150-300g grated Cheddar cheese
- salt and pepper to taste

Serves 6

Method

1. Arrange chips on one big platter or on individual plates.
2. Mix shallots, pepper, jalapeños and tomatoes well in a bowl.
3. Add diced chicken.
4. Spoon on top of chips.
5. Sprinkle cheese over each one.
6. Microwave on a medium-high setting, each plate for about 2-3 minutes, or a large platter for around 5-6 minutes.

Steamed Vegetables

I've always liked vegetables, never had to be encouraged to eat my carrots because it would allow me to see in the dark (certainly not true for me), or eat my greens or salad stuff.

So it was something of a surprise when one day I bought a steamer (it was reduced to an irresistable price) and discovered that it added a whole new dimension to my usual vegetables.

I don't steam meat or fish, but my steamer is now one of my best used pieces of kitchen equipment for cooking cabbage, cauliflower and broccoli – those vegetables which so easily lose their crispness and flavour when cooked in water, becoming little more than mush, retain shape and flavour in the steamer, and it's so easy to throw a mix of veg in together to cook.

Ingredients

Vegetables
Your usual amounts of cabbage, cauliflower or broccoli or a combination of carrot (sliced into battons)/cauliflower/ broccoli. You can add celery, sliced peppers or whole mushrooms. Steaming lets individual vegetables retain their own flavours.
For additional interest you can add a cooked garnish.

For broccoli:
• 1 onion, sliced
• 2 tomatoes, chopped

For cauliflower:
• a handful of cashew nuts
• 2 spring onions, sliced
• grated Parmesan cheese

For cabbage:
• 1 onion chopped
• cream
• good knob of butter
• wholegrain mustard

Method

1. Prepare vegetables as usual and cook in steamer for required time according to amount and steamer guidelines. Don't add salt or other seasonings. These can be added when cooked or in garnishes.
2. Meanwhile prepare garnish.

For broccoli:
3. Sweat onion in a little oil. When softened add chopped tomatoes and cook until softened. Season and add some chopped parsely or basil. Pour over broccoli and serve.

For cauliflower:
4. Cook cashew nuts in a little oil until lightly browned. Add spring onions, seasoning and some dried or fresh herbs. Pour over cauliflower and grate some Parmesan cheese over top.

For cabbage:
5. Sweat chopped onion in the butter. Add cream and a good spoonful of wholegrain mustard (see recipe on page 134). Pour over cabbage and enjoy.

Roast Asparagus with Parmesan

Ingredients

- 450g asparagus
- 6-8 tablespoons olive oil
- coarse sea salt
- freshly grated parmesan

Asparagus is a part of the lily family, similar to onions, leeks and garlic, and was first cultivated about 2,500 years ago in Greece.

Even today asparagus is mainly grown in sunny climates where rain is less frequent than in Scotland. But in recent years a few courageous and determined suppliers have successfully, but not without challenges, grown asparagus for the commercial market, producing crops with a flavour just as good or perhaps even better than asparagus grown elsewhwere. This is attributed to the slower growth of the plant, spending more time in the Scottish sun.

The season for asparagus is short, only six weeks from the beginning of May to mid June, so take advantage of it.

Method

1. Preheat the oven to gas mark 4/350°F/180°C
2. Cut the woody stems off the asparagus.
3. Generously oil a large ovenproof dish or roasting tin (big enough to take the asparagus in a tight single layer).
4. Sprinkle coarse sea salt lightly over the base.
5. Arrange the asparagus on top and drizzle over the remaining olive oil, erring on the generous side.
6. Turn the asparagus with your hands to coat them nicely in oil.
7. Sprinkle with a little more salt.
8. Roast for 10-18 minutes until tender.
9. Scatter with parmesan if you wish, and serve immediately.

Roasted Aubergines

I must have been quite old before I tasted my first aubergines. They certainly weren't part of the mince and tattie regime. But travel abroad and membership of the European Union has brought about a change in our buying and eating habits. Aubergines, as well as being a tasty vegetable dish on their own, are great at bulking out stew and pasta dishes where the meat is a little thin on the plate.

Aubergines must be one of the most eyecatching vegetables with their glossy dark purple skins. Because of their shape, I assume, in some countries they are called egg plants, though to me they are not egg shaped. What they do have is a flavour all of their own.

For me they are a potent reminder of relaxed meals on sun-warmed Greek islands.

Ingredients

- Half an aubergine per person
- 2 or three cloves garlic cut into quarters
- olive oil
- salt and pepper

Alternatively:
substitute pesto for some of the olive oil

Method

1. Preheat oven to 200ºC.
2. Wash aubergines and cut in half lengthways.
3. Place on baking tray or baking dish skin side down.
4. Make a few slits in aubergine flesh and tuck garlic slivers into them.
5. Drizzle aubergines generously with olive oil and sprinkle with salt and pepper.
Alternatively spread with some pesto and then drizzle with some oil.
6. Bake for about 30 minutes. About halfway through drizzle on more oil or, if watching the calories, cover with aluminium foil.
7. Enjoy with cooked meats or indeed on their own.
Alternatively scoop flesh from skin to make an aubergine dip.

Cauliflower and Tomato Crumble

As a child I was always told to eat my greens but actually this really just meant carrots, peas, turnip, cabbage and my favourite, cauliflower. Artichokes, asparagus, celery, peppers, fennel, courgettes and aubergines were not available in our local green-grocers. It is good to see today's children tuck into celery sticks at their birthday parties.

When I asked my grandson what he had for tea one time he said, "Oh, we had an aubergine dish again!" And of course we have recipes for carrot cake, courgette, carrot and pear cake, and my favourite chocolate and beetroot.

Ingredients

- 1 head of cauliflower
- 4 tomatoes sliced
- salt and pepper
- 1 teasp fresh thyme leaves or 1/2 teaspoon dried

Sauce
- 50g butter
- 50g plain flour
- ¾ pint of milk

Crumble
- 100g plain flour
- 50g rolled oats
- 50g Cheddar Cheese
- salt
- freshly ground pepper
- 100g butter

Method

1. Cook the cauliflower in salted, boiling water, or steam, until almost tender.
2. Pack tightly in a highly buttered , heatproof dish.
Sauce
3. Melt the butter for the sauce, stir in the flour.
4. Cook the roux for a couple of minutes.
5. Add the milk then whisk until smooth.
6. Pour over the cauliflower.
7. Cover with tomato slices.
8. Sprinkle with thyme leaves, salt and pepper.
9. Preheat the oven to gas mark 6, 400ºF, 200ºC.
Crumble
10. Mix the flour, oats, grated cheese, salt and pepper.
11. Melt the butter and stir into the crumbly mixture.
12. Cool slightly then scatter over vegetables in a thick layer.
13. Bake for about 30minutes until the crumble is golden brown and crisp.
14. Serve immediately.

Paprika Potato Wedges

"You mean there are ways of cooking potatoes other than chips?" asked an acquaintance some years ago. I assumed she was kidding, but maybe not. I had an aunt who served chips to her family every evening – deep fried as that was in the days before oven chips.

My mother used to make fritters with potato slices dipped in batter and deep fried, and mashed potatoes was a favourite with lashings of gravy. I occasionally make duchess potatoes – mashed with the addition of egg yolks and nutmeg. I omit the fiddly piping into shapes and just do it in an oven dish. This is another potato recipe popular in our house, and makes a change from boiled.

Originating in the Andes, the potato is now an important crop for Scotland, recognised within the EU as a Community Grade region for seed potato production.

Ingredients

- sufficient largish potatoes for the number you are feeding
- vegetable or sunflower oil
- rosemary (fresh or dried)
- paprika
- salt and pepper

I sometimes add a couple of onions, quartered, to the potato wedges.

Method

1. Wash the potatoes. I leave the skins on.
2. Cut into wedges.
3. Put into roasting tin and drizzle well with the the oil. Get your hands in and ensure the wedges are well covered.
4. Sprinkle liberally with the rosemary and paprika ensuring not just the top of the wedges are coated.
5. Season with salt and pepper.
6. Roast in the oven – 200ºC or 180ºC if a fan oven for about 45 minutes or until wedges are cooked.

Daifuku Mochi

Daifuku Mochi is rice cake with Anko, sweet red bean paste, inside. It is a traditional but very popular Japanese sweet, first made almost 700 years ago, but not as a sweet dessert. Then, sugar was rare, but Daifuku became more like today's when sugar was more readily available to people 200 years later.

Mochi is a Japanese sticky rice cake used in savoury and sweet dishes. Mochi is usually made from sweet rice, cooked and pounded until a very sticky paste, then formed into cakes or blocks.

Japanese art influenced Impressionist painters and many Scottish artists, including Charles Rennie Mackintosh. Many collected Japanese woodblock prints and blue and white pottery. Now Japanese cuisine, such as sushi, has become equally fashionable.

Ingredients

- 1 cup mochiko (sweet rice flour) (160g)
- ¾ cup water (180ml)
- ¾ cup sugar (150g)
- katakuriko (potato starch) or cornstarch
- Aanko (half the recipe)

Anko is a sweet paste that can be made from beans, chestnuts, sesame, sweet potatoes, and sometimes fruit. Despite this variety, it's most commonly used to mean "red bean paste" made from azuki beans. To make anko from azuki, the beans are simmered, and then mixed with sugar to produce a paste.

Mochiko and Anko can be bought at Japanese or Asian supermarkets, or online.

Method

1. Mix mochiko and water in a glass (or other heat proof bowl) and mix well.
2. Add some more water if it's too dry, 1 tablespoon at a time.
3. Steam the mochiko dough (leaving the dough in the bowl) in a steamer for 20 minutes.
4. Transfer the steamed mochi into a pot and cook at medium to medium low heat with a third of the sugar (1/4 cup).
5. When the sugar is completely dissolved, add another third of the sugar and mix well. Add the last part of the sugar and cook some more until the sugar is dissolved. Take the time to melt the sugar, but be careful not to burn it.
6. Take the hot mochi out from the pot onto a sheet pan liberally dusted with katakuriko or cornstarch.
7. Cut some mochi out, and wrap the mochi around a ball of anko (size of a heaped tablespoon). Pinch the end of Mochi to seal. Serve it with the seam side down.

Doubly Delicious

Cranachan – my husband's Granny's favourite. A traditional sweet served by the better off, or those owning a cow, or on special occasions. Trifle may have ruled the roost of Scottish sweets, but Cranachan deserves a place at the top table too. Simple and almost instant to make.

Yiaourti me meli – No Cream? Okay, then hopefully you have that never-to- be-without ingredient – yogurt, and hopefully Greek or Turkish yogurt which are less sharp and very like cream. I was served this as a special dish one gloriously warm evening by a Romanian waitress in a little open-air restaurant in Pefkos, Rhodes while she chatted animatedly to me about her son back in Romania and her life in Greece.

Ingredients

Cranachan
- ½pint double cream
- 3-4 ozs pinhead oatmeal
- sugar (to taste)
- 4-6 ozs raspberries
- flavouring (eg vanilla essence) or 1 tablespoon of whisky

Yiaourti me meli (Greek Yogurt and honey)
- Greek yogurt
- good quality honey (the Greeks use thyme honey)
- walnuts

No quantities as presumably it depended on what was available. So judge according to your taste.

Cranachan

Yiaourti me meli

Method

Cranachan

1. Lightly toast the pinhead oatmeal in a dry frying pan or in oven until slightly brown and nutty tasting. By far the best oatmeal is Hogarth's of Kelso.

2. While the oatmeal is toasting whip some cream until fluffy, adding a little sugar and flavouring/booze to taste.

3. Spoon into dishes, sprinkle with the toasted oatmeal and top with raspberries. If raspberries are not available, then experiment with fresh fruit (bananas, clementines, grapes, strawberries), or maybe tinned cherries.

Yiaourti me meli

1. Spoon yogurt into dishes, drizzle with runny honey and top with walnuts. Amazing how good this is.

2. Instead of walnuts you could try other nuts. I've substituted crushed almonds and added nectarine segments and it still tasted extraordinarily good. You could try the toasted oatmeal to give a nutty flavour, and the raspberries.

Both can be served with shortbread or an amaretti biscuit.

89

Zanzibar Coconut Icecream

Zanzibar has always been known by travellers as the Spice Island.

The evening breezes bring in the wonderful scent of the wild spices from the forests.

This recipe that uses local spices is a favourite on the island.

Sir John Kirk, was a Scottish physician, naturalist, companion to explorer Dr David Livingstone (whom he accompanied on the Second Zambezi Expedition as a botanist), and British administrator (he was appointed British Consul in Zanzibar where he was instrumental in ending the slave trade).

Kirk introduced a very distinct and pretty species of orchid to the United Kingdom, subsequently named Angaecum Scottianum.

Ingredients

- 2 x 14 oz cans full fat coconut milk
- 1 x 14 oz can condensed milk
- 1 x 14 oz can evaporated milk
- 1 teaspoon grated nutmeg or cardamom powder
- 1 teaspoon rose water essence
- A little sugar if required but do not make it too sweet.
- A little shredded coconut and a sprig of mint to garnish.

Method

1. Put all ingredients in a large bowl or a blender and mix well.
2. Freeze until ice crystals begin to form.
3. Remove from the freezer and mix until the crystals have broken down then whisk till the mixture is fluffy.
4. Put the mixture in a container with a cover and freeze until solid. Keep checking to make sure crystals don't form again. If so mix again.
5. Remove the ice cream about 5 minutes before serving to allow it to soften a little. Garnish with a little shredded coconut and a sprig of mint.

Marshmallow Delight & Date Balls

Marshmallow Delight is a recipe my mother made for my brothers and I when we were small. I had forgotten all about it until my neighbour showed me a cookery book she had been sent from Australia by her penpal. They had kept in touch for 70 years. The cookery book raised money for Cunnamulla Branch of the Queensland Cancer Fund.

The second recipe is also Australian and was found in a little homemade book presented by the Auxiliary of the Blue Nursing Service Stanthorpe.

The links between Scotland and Australia stretch back to the first British expedition of the Endeavour commanded by Lieutenant James Cook, son of a Scottish ploughman. Cook landed at Botany Bay in April 1770, with the first Scottish settlers arriving in Australia in 1788.

Ingredients

- 1 large pkt of marshmallows
- double or whipping cream
- 1 tin of pineapple rings

Date Balls
- 2 eggs beaten
- ½ cup margarine
- 225g dates finely sliced
- 1½ cups of Rice Crispies
- ½ cup of chopped nuts
- 1 teaspoon of vanilla essence
- coconut for covering

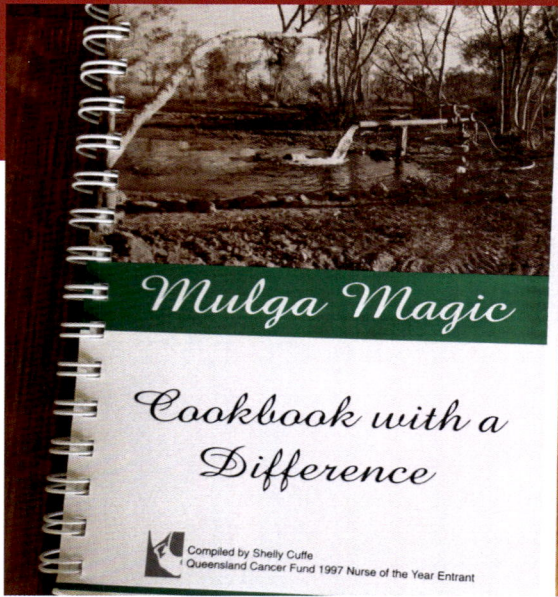

Method

1. Using scissors snip the marshmallows into small pieces then cut the pineapple rings into bite sized bits.
2. Whip the cream until thick.
3. Add the marshmallows and the pineapple. If too thick add a little juice from the pineapple.
4. Chill before serving.

You can substitute other fruits eg Passion fruit or strawberries. Goes well with jelly.

Date Balls
1. Combine eggs, margarine, and dates and cook over low heat stirring constantly.
2. Boil for 2 minutes.
3. Remove from heat and add the Rice Crispies, chopped nuts and vanilla.
4. Cool. Shape into little balls. Roll in coconut.

93

Cranberry & Oatmeal Wholemeal Bread

I spent a year living just outside of Boston, Massachusetts, which is a huge cranberry-growing state, contributing over $100m to the economy and employing over 6,000 people.

I liked the idea of fusing Scottish oatmeal with new England cranberries, so that's how this recipe was born. The oatmeal has a delicious nutty taste which compliments the sweet cranberries really well. It makes for much more interesting toast in the morning, and cheese sandwiches with this bread are simply sublime!

Ingredients

- 500g wholemeal flour (plain, not self-raising)
- 30g dried cranberries (or otherwise to taste)
- 300ml warm water
- 2 tablespoons of Scottish oatmeal
- 1 sachet of dried bread yeast
- 1 egg
- 1 teaspoon of salt
- 1 teaspoon sugar (plain white is fine, demerara or brown adds nice caramel flavour)

Method

If you've got a bread maker, this is a cinch – just throw every-thing into it, using dough setting, and leave it to do the work.

Otherwise:
1. Mix all the dry ingredients and cranberries together in a bowl (leave aside 1 tablespoon of the oatmeal – this will be for your crust later).
2. Beat the egg in a small bowl making sure you get lots of air into it. 30 seconds work with a fork should do nicely.
3. Add the egg to the mix and the 300ml of water.
4. Get stuck in with your hands and mix the liquid into flour.
5. Keep going until the bowl sides are clean of flour and you have a solid ball of consistent dough. You want it just a little bit sticky – if you've still got dry flour in the bowl, just add a little more water and work it in.
6. Cover the bowl and leave in a nice warm place to prove for about an hour. The yeast should roughly double the size of the dough ball.

7. Pre-heat your oven to 200ºC.

8. Drop the dough ball out onto a clean, dry surface.

9. Knead the dough to fold in some more air and make sure the cranberries and oatmeal are evenly distributed.

10. Shape the dough into a slightly flat cylinder about 10 inches long.

11. Spread your remaining tablespoon of oatmeal evenly onto your working surface, and then roll your dough through it letting it pick up all the oatmeal. If the consistency is right, it should pretty much clean the surface.

12. You can use a bread tin, but personally I just bake it on a flat sheet. Dust your tin or baking sheet with flour to prevent sticking, and transfer your dough to it.

13. As a final step, take a sharp knife and cut diagonal lines through the dough about three-quarters of an inch deep, spaced evenly along its length. This will help get heat into the centre of the loaf, give you a pleasing aesthetic, and help to make a lovely crunchy crust.

14. Place in oven and bake for 30-40 minutes. You'll know it is ready when any cranberries exposed on the surface go brown.

15. Remove from oven and transfer to a wire grill or pot stand to cool (if you leave it on a flat surface the base may go a bit soggy as the steam condenses).

16. Serve with your favourite spread, or as a personal recommendation, salami and brie.

17. Enjoy!

The beautiful Berwickshire coastline is ever colourful, and ever changing from rocky to sandy, cliffs to hidden bays, home to a vast array of wildlife and wide, open views.

Slicing "Focaccia" Bread

This one started life as an onion bread, and quickly evolved to include olives, mushrooms and tomatoes. It's almost what you'd get if you tipped the ingredients for a homemade pizza into the breadmaker, which is not far off what you get! It is quite a lot of work though, so we tend to reserve this one for special occasions. The olives give it a wonderful strong flavour, and the bread is soft and moist while incredibly filling. Toasted and served with pate, it makes for a novel and tasty starter.

All the bread we eat is home made. Once you have tried it, the flavour and texture becomes addictive – far superior and more satisfying than anything bought.

So, go on, try it.

Ingredients

- 500g strong plain white flour (not self-raising!)
- 200ml warm water
- 100ml olive oil
- 100g olives (any variety, – I use green pitted)
- 100g cherry tomatoes (for nice sweet flavour, but regular tomatoes will do)
- 1-2 mushrooms (optional)
- 1 large red onion (white onions are fine)
- 3 teaspoons dried mixed herbs (or fresh, if you've got them)
- 2 teaspoons of dried bread yeast (or sachets if that's what you've got)
- 1 egg
- 2 teaspoons sugar (plain white is fine, demerara or brown adds nice caramel flavour)
- 1 teaspoon of salt

Method

This isn't the classic tear-and-share Italian bread, but a derivitive adapted for slicing and the Scandanavian-style open sandwiches preferred in my household. But trust me – the taste is epic.

A bit of background:
There's a LOT of veg to mix into this, so give it a double-dose of yeast to promote rising otherwise it will turn out like a brick. The strong olive aroma and flavour will mask any "yeastiness" - at least, I certainly couldn't detect any.

So let's get on with it
1. Finely chop the onion (and optional mushroom) and pan fry in olive oil until caramelised (that's "just lightly burnt" in non-chef parlance).
2. Leave aside to cool.
3. If you've got a bread maker, it will do a lot of work for you – you need only roughly chop the olives and tomatoes and

the breadmaker's mixing action will break them down quite nicely. If you're doing the mixing by hand, you'll want to chop the ingredients much more finely.

Otherwise:

1. Mix all the dry ingredients together in a bowl.
2. Beat the egg in a small bowl making sure you get lots of air into it.
3. Add the egg, water, and chopped veg to the mix, and get in with your hands. You want to make sure that the veg is fairly evenly distributed and that you have a solid ball of consistent dough.
4. Cover the bowl and leave in a nice warm place to prove for about an hour. The yeast should roughly double the size of the dough ball.
5. Pre-heat your oven to 200ºC.
6. Drop the dough ball out onto a clean, dry surface.
7. Knead to fold in some more air and make sure the veg is evenly distributed.
8. Shape the dough into a slightly flat cylinder about 10 inches long, and place it on a baking sheet dusted with flour. You can optionally add some grated cheese to the top of the loaf at this point.
9. Place in oven and bake for 30-40 minutes, and wonder at the marvellous aroma!
10. Enjoy!

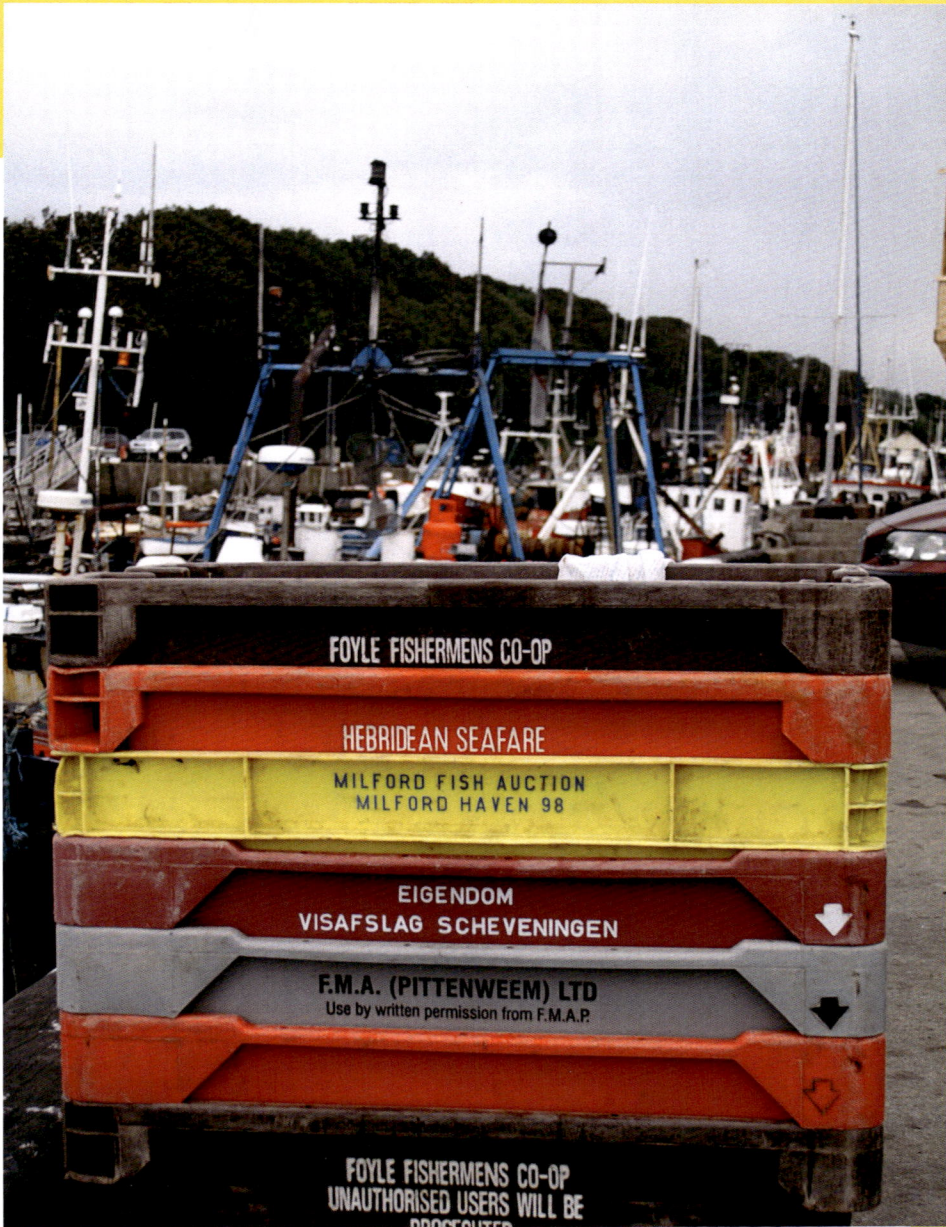

The international aspect of fishing and fish processing is indicated by these fish boxes, an aspect which may change dramatically after the UK leaves the European Union.

Madeiran Bolo do Caco

Ingredients

Bolo do Caco is a staple bread of Madeira. It uses sweet potato because of a lack of cereals on the island.

Traditionally, the Bolo do Caco is baked on a basalt stone heated at high temperature, directly on hot embers. This stone is called caco, hence the name of this (soda scone-like) bread. Today, cast iron plates or non-stick heavy-bottom pans often replace the original slab.

Bolo do Caco are sold widely from street stalls as well as in supermarkets and we found them ideal for filling sandwiches, stuffed with cold meat, cheese, salad they didn't go soggy like ordinary bread.

Bolo do Caco reminds me so much of my mother's soda scones. Not sure why but if you try the Bola do Caco you might understand.

- 750g sweet potato
- 1 kg flour
- around 150mls warmed water
- 25g baker's yeast
- pinch of salt
- garlic butter and parsley

Method

1. Peel the sweet potatoes. Cut into large pieces and place in a saucepan. Cover with water, bring to boil and cook covered for 20 minutes over medium-high heat.
2. Drain and mash them.
3. Mix yeast and water and add salt.
4. Pour flour into a large baking bowl. Scoop a well in centre and add mashed sweet potato and yeast mixture. Mix well.
5. Knead until dough is elastic.
6. Cover with a clean cloth and let the dough ferment for 2 to 3 hours.
7. Dust work surface with flour and divide dough into portions, shape into rounds and flatten out.
8. Rest for 30 minutes in a warm place, protected from drafts.
9. Heat a dry pan over medium-high heat and cook the bolos do caco on both sides until browned and a thin and slightly hard crust is formed. Turn regularly and using tongs take each bolo do caco and turn them on the hot pan to bake the sides.
10. Serve warm with salted garlic butter and parsley.

My Mother's Soda Scones

Ingredients

My mother made these on a regular basis. In modern parlance they were her signature dish. On Sunday afternoons my grandparents came to visit, as did aunts and older cousins who usually brought their latest boyfriend to see if he passed the 'family' test – a nervewracking experience for them, puir sowels.

Anyway, as soon as the doorbell rang out came the big, circular cast iron girdle with the 'D' shaped handle and loop for hanging over a range fire. On to the gas cooker it went while the ingredients were thrown into a baking bowl. Before visitors knew what was happening they were handed a scone dripping with butter. One pregnant cousin ate so many we worried about the child, but she turned out relatively normal!

Our dog loved the soda scones too.

- 1lb flour
- 2 level teaspoons salt
- 2 level teaspoons bicarbonate of soda
- 4 level teaspoons cream of tartar
- ½ pint of milk
- 1 ozs fat (optional)

I don't remember my mother using fat, but you can experiment and decide what you like best.

Best eaten whilst still warm with lashings of butter that melts and dribbles down your chin.

Method

1. Heat the girdle slowly, or nowadays it would probably be a heavy-based frying pan or a plate on your cooker.
2. Sieve all dry ingredients.
3. Rub in fat if wanted.
4. Add milk and mix to a light elastic dough.
5. Divide dough into three or four pieces.
6. Roll our on floured surface and cut into four.
7. Cook on fairly hot girdle, allowing 3 or 4 minutes per side.
8. Cool in a tea towel.

(Gluten free and vegan) Molly's Magical Marbled Muffins

Molly lives with her brother and other animals on the edge of mystical Dartmoor in Devon.

She loves all things magical – from fairies, glitter and crystals to Harry Potter and The Velveteen Rabbit. (Her patronus is, of course, a rabbit!).

Because of the distance from the Borders, Molly's grandparents don't see enough of her or her big brother.

It is estimated the number of Scots adopting a vegan diet has surged in recent years with up to 350,000 Scots now eating plant-based diets, and shunning meat, dairy and egg products.

According to the Vegan Society Veganism is a way of living which seeks to exclude, as far as possible and practicable, all forms of exploitation of, and cruelty to, animals for food, clothing or any other purpose.

Ingredients

- ¾ cup rice flour
- ¾ cup ground almonds
- ⅓ cup coconut
- ⅓ cup brown sugar
- 1 teaspoon baking soda
- 1 teaspoon baking powder
- pinch sea salt
- ⅔ cup almond milk
- ⅓ cup coconut oil, melted
- 2 teaspoons apple cider vinegar
- 1 teaspoon vanilla extract
- zest of 1 large orange
- 1 teaspoon cinnamon
- ⅓ cup cocoa/cacao powder
- ⅓ cup water

For creamy lemon frosting:
- 40g creamed coconut
- ⅓ cup hot water
- zest of 1 organic, unwaxed lemon
- 2 tablespoons lemon juice
- 1 tablespoon icing sugar/ 2 tbsp maple syrup

Method

1. Preheat oven to 180ºC (160ºC fan assisted)/ 350ºF
2. In large bowl, mix together the rice flour, ground almonds, sugar, baking powder, baking soda and salt.
3. Pour in the oil, milk, apple cider vinegar and vanilla extract. Whisk to combine. The consistency should be just pourable, but not runny.
4. Split half mixture into another bowl, and add the cocoa and water - combine and whisk until the consistency is the same.
5. Into first bowl, whisk in the orange zest and cinnamon.
6. Line a muffin tin with paper cases - about 9.
7. Dollop alternate spoonfuls of chocolate and orange mixtures into each case. Drag cocktail stick through to swirl together.
8. Bake for about 15-20 minutes, then cool the muffins in their cases on a wire tray. When completely cool, add the frosting made by blending all the frosting ingredients together and adjusting according to taste and consistency required.
9. Dollop frosting into each muffin and add sprinkles for extra magic. Yum!

Biscotti

Biscotti reminds me of a family visit to Italy to stay with my brother and his family. We crossed Lago Maggiore on the ferry, drove up a very steep winding road into the mountains and arrived at the village of Gurro. Why were we visiting? Why did the village have a Scottish Association Bar where kilt wearing Italians sip espresso and enjoy a biscotti? Why do they have a strange, incomprehensible dialect, use 800 words of Gaelic origin and love playing the bagpipes? Why are some villagers called Gibi or Donaldi with the surname of MacDonald? Well, Gurro was populated 500 years ago by Scottish mercenaries forced to retreat to the town because of the onset of winter after the Battle of Pavia. The area reminded them of their native Highlands so stay they did.

Ingredients

- 200g plain flour
- 1 teaspoon baking powder
- 80g golden caster sugar
- 50g dessiccated coconut (or ground almonds)
- 100g mixed fruit
- 80g glace cherries, halved
- 3g nuts such as almonds, brazils, or cashews roughly chopped
- 2 eggs beaten

Makes 12 Slices

Visit Gurro on the second Sunday in July when the town celebrates with their tartan and march to the bagpipes. You can watch while enjoying an espresso and a biscotti.

Method

1. Preheat oven to 180ºC/gas mark 4
2. Line two baking trays
3. In large bowl mix together flour, baking powder, caster sugar, coconut (or ground almonds), mixed fruit, cherries and nuts.
4. Gradually add eggs and mix until a dough forms, using hands to combine if necessary. If the dough is too wet add a little more flour
5. Shape dough into a log and place on a lined baking sheet, flattening it until approximately 4cm thick and 20-25cm long
6. Bake for 25mins. Remove from oven and reduce temperature to 160ºC/ gas mark 3
7. Let dough cool for about 10 minutes, then use a serrated knife and cut at an angle into about 2cm slices.
8 Place on trays and return to oven for 20 minutes to dry out.
9. Allow to cool completely.
10. Serve with a cup of coffee (and dunk!).

Brussels Loaf

My grandmother liked nothing better than to have her family around her, so every Wednesday was her 'at home' day. Members of the family who could make it descended on my grand-parent's two room and kitchen flat. Invariably the food was mince and macaroni – an elastic meal was the way she described it. Those arriving early got a good helping of mince coating their macaroni. Later arrivals found on their plates more macaroni afloat on diluted mince gravy. But we didn't complain. It was the mingling, the news and gossip everyone went for.

My mother and her sisters inherited this love of family parties and get-togethers. I remember them as numerous. Brussels Loaf was a favourite on many of these occasions.

Ingredients

- 4 ozs margarine (or butter if you want)
- 1 cup of milk
- 1 cup of sugar
- 2 cups mixed dried fruit
- 1 tablespoon syrup
- 1 tablespoon treacle
- 1 egg
- 2½ cups self raising flour

The women in my life – my mother, her sisters and sister-in-law and my grand-mother.

Method

1. Melt margarine, milk, and sugar in pan.
2. Add fruit and mix. Leave to cool
3. Add syrup and treacle, the egg (lightly whipped) and flour. Mix together.
4. Grease and line a baking tin with greaseproof paper.
5. Bake in a moderate oven 375ºF for 1¼ hours until springy to the touch and coming away from sides of tin.

An easy and quick to make fruit loaf that's a favourite with family and friends.

111

Gran's Currant Bun
Her Black Bun for Ne'erday

Whilst looking for recipes for this book I unearthed a little black book belonging to my gran. It was lined up as a cash book but she had used it to write down a few recipes. The calendars at the front of the notebook are for 1937 and 1938 – so eighty years ago, in another age.

My gran possibly had basic, but not very accurate, kitchen scales, though I never saw her use them. Quantities were judged by experience.

No precise oven temperatures for her. Until I was a teenager she used a coal burning range which my grandad religiously black-leaded every Friday evening. I can still see her in her floral smock and dangly earrings, a smile on her face, her hair done in silvery coils like a judge's wig, stirring pots of soup, or making some other meal on the gas hob of the range.

Ingredients

The Crust
- 3 cups of flour
- 4 ozs butter
- ½ teaspoon cream of tartar

The Bun Mixture
- 1 lb flour
- 1 bare teaspoon cream of tartar (the mind boggles envisaging a bare tea spoon!)
- 1 bare teaspoon baking soda
- 8 ozs sugar
- 2 lbs currants
- 4 ozs chopped peel
- 4 ozs almonds
- ½ oz ground ginger
- ½ oz cinnamon
- milk

currant bun

The crust.
3 cups of flour
¼ lb butter
½ teasp cream of tartar
mix latter with flour
rub in butter & make
into firm dough with
water. roll thin, grease
tin & line with dough
keeping a piece for top.
The Bun mixture
1 lb flour
1 bare teasp cr of tartar
1 " " baking soda
¼ lb sugar
2 " currants
4 oz chopped peel

CALENDAR for 1937

JANUARY	FEBRUARY	MARCH	APRIL
MAY	JUNE	JULY	AUGUST
SEPTEMBER	OCTOBER	NOVEMBER	DECEMBER

CALENDAR for 1938

JANUARY	FEBRUARY	MARCH	APRIL
MAY	JUNE	JULY	AUGUST
SEPTEMBER	OCTOBER	NOVEMBER	DECEMBER

Method

The Crust
1. Mix cream of tartar with flour.
2. Rub in butter and knead into firm dough with water.
3. Roll thin.
4. Grease tin (no size given) and line with dough keeping a piece for top.

The Bun Mixture
5. Mix all ingredients well with just enough milk to moisten the whole.
6. Put in pastry lined tin and smooth top.
7. Wet pastry edges and cover with pastry lid, pressing edges well together.
8. Prick all over with fork.
9. Brush with white of egg.
10. Bake in a steady oven for 2½ hours. (About 350°F I would guess.)

Kathi's Chocolate Cake

When I first came to Edinburgh to study English in the early 90s, cooking and baking familiar dishes became an important link to my country bumpkin upbringing in East Germany. I've always loved cake but what Scotland had to offer at the time just didn't cut the mustard! Thankfully I had appreciative friends and flatmates to share my baking with and meeting up with them years later it seems they remember me most by my cheesecake! The recipe here, however, is the one I get asked about the most, a chocolate cake recipe which I originally acquired off a German friend. I have altered it beyond recognition since, changing and tweaking the ingredients every time I used it until I thought it would do.

Ingredients

Chocolate Cake
- 250g margarine
- 1½ cups of sugar (1 cup = 250ml)
- ½ cup cocoa powder
- ½ cup water
- 3 eggs
- 200g self-raising flour
- ½ tsp baking powder
- vanilla essence

Optional Icing
- 100g of dark chocolate
- 50g unsalted butter

I like this cake because it uses cocoa powder instead of melted chocolate, much cheaper and easier to use. In our house there are two versions of this, the "everyday" version which is the plain chocolate sponge and the "birthday" version, with a layer of apricot jam in the middle and chocolate icing/decorations on top.

Method

Chocolate Cake
1. Melt the margarine in a large pot on a medium heat.
2. Add the sugar, cocoa powder and water.
3. Using a hand whisk, combine all ingredients until the sugar has melted and there are no lumps of any sort.
4. Let the mixture cool somewhat before whisking in the eggs and vanilla essence.
5. Sift the flour into the mix whilst whisking continuously.
6. Pour into a leak-proof greased 9 inch round spring-form cake tin and bake at 160ºC (fan) for 50 minutes.
7. Turn out and when cool dust with icing sugar.

Optional icing
8. Melt the butter and chocolate in a double boiler (or carefully in a pan over a very low heat).
9. Stir until it is all melted and well combined.
10. Pour onto your cake and smooth with a pallet knife.
11. Get your kids to decorate it.

Mum's Paradise Squares

Brexit is a subject you can't escape these days, even in this cookbook. Brexiters ask what is wrong with leaving the EU, returning to the days before we joined – the 1970s? Well, I remember the 1970s – strikes the three day week, powercuts to conserve energy with two toddlers suddenly finding themselves in the dark. I kept a torch in my pocket so I could find them. Coal shortages – one bag a week because I had young kids. It took nearly a bag to get our stove going – it heated the water and the house. So we had to pile on clothes. Brrrr!

But there were happier times too, though no-one viewing my mother's kitchen in the above photo would now aspire to that. What we eat has changed, lifestyles have changed. There is no going back.

Ingredients

- Short crust pastry to fill a rectangular baking tray (probably 8ozs)
- 4 ozs margarine (or butter)
- 4 ozs caster sugar
- 1 egg
- 1 teacup sultanas
- 2 tablespoons glacé cherries
- 2 tablespoons walnuts
- 2 tablespoons ground rice
- 1 tablespoon ground almonds
- a few drops almond essence
- raspberry jam

Return to the past.

Method

1. Make shortcrust pastry and line a rectangular baking tin with it.
2. Spread with some raspberry jam.
3. Cream margarine (or butter) with sugar.
4. Drop in egg and beat well.
5. Mix the sultanas, cherries, walnuts, ground rice, ground almonds and stir into mixture, ensuring all is well mixed.
6. Flavour with almond essence.
7. Pour on top of pastry base and smooth.
8. Bake for 30-35 minutes at 375°F until firm.
9. Leave till cold. Cut into squares or fingers and sprinkle with sugar.
10. Enjoy.

Microwave Dumpling

We lived for many years in Dalmally in Argyll, only moving to the Borders when we retired as it was the nearest we could get to a mid-way point between our family in Scotland and the south of England.

When I was young I never got a cake for my birthday. My mother always used to make me a dumpling. I still make one occasionally, and my husband loves eating it the next day fried or with butter.

It didn't always have to be a birthday that prompted the making of a dumpling, some stale bread in the bread bin was often sufficient excuse to throw the ingredients into a bowl.

This is a recipe I was given when in Argyll. It really is a very good substitute for the traditional dumpling and so easy and quick to make.

Ingredients

- ½ pint water
- ¾ cup sugar
- ½ lb sultanas
- ½ lb raisins
- 4 oz margarine or butter
- 1 tablespoon treacle
- 1 teaspoon mixed spice
- 1 teaspoon cinnamon
- 1 teaspoon bicarbonate of soda
- 8 oz plain flour
- 2 beaten eggs

A modern take on the traditional home made clootie dumpling.

Method

1. Put the water, sugar, sultanas, raisins, margarine or butter, treacle, mixed spice and cinnamon into a pot and simmer for 1 minute.
2. Line a Pyrex casserole with cling film.
3. Place flour and bicarbonate of soda in a bowl and add fruit mixture and lastly eggs.
4. Place mixture into the lined Pyrex casserole dish. DO NOT COVER.
5. Place in microwave for 9¾ minutes – 600w microwave (less time for higher wattage microwaves)
6. Bring out and leave to cool for a while, then turn out onto a plate.
P.S. Takes ages to cool.

Traditional Clootie Dumpling

For many of us a dumpling took the place of birthday, Christmas or other celebration cake, or was sometimes just made on a miserable winter day to cheer everyone up.

We always enjoyed it on its own, occasionally with a little milk, never with custard, although others perhaps served it like that.

There was always enough left for another day when it could be fried and served with sugar sprinkled over it. No wonder Scots' health was bad! But it was warming food for a damp, chilly climate and houses with no central heating, just a kitchen range, and, in my grandparents' case, no hot running water.

My gran used to have little charms or tiny white china figures that were wrapped in a twist of greaseproof paper and inserted into the mixture. She always ensured the kids found a lucky charm in their slice.

Ingredients

- 1 lb 4 ozs self-raising flour
- 9 oz currants
- 9 oz sultanas
- 4¼ oz shredded beef suet (vegetarian suet is now available and can be used instead)
- 3¾ oz dried breadcrumbs
- 7 oz caster sugar
- 1 egg, lightly beaten
- 4 fl oz milk
- 1 teaspoon mixed spice
- 1 teaspoon baking powder
- a pinch salt
- 1 tablespoon golden syrup
- 1 tablespoon treacle

Dumpling makers par excellence: left – my mum; right – my gran

Method

1. Bring a large soup pot of water to the boil.
2 Using a large baking bowl, combine flour, currants, sultanas, suet, breadcrumbs and sugar.
3. Mix egg and milk with mixed spice, baking powder, salt, golden syrup and treacle.
4. Stir into flour mixture to form a wet dough.
5. Scald a linen or cotton cloth (my mother kept a dumpling cloth, stained with age) by dipping in boiling water.
6. Sprinkle liberally with flour. Place dumpling mixture in centre of cloth, draw edges together to form a ball, leaving room for the dumpling to expand, and tie firmly with string.
7. Place the dumpling into the boiling water (my mother always placed an old plate on the bottom of the pot – not sure why), reduce heat to a low boil and cook for 3½ hours, adding more boiling water as required.
8. Remove dumpling from the water, remove cloth and dry dumpling in front of a fire or in a 150º C/gas mark 2 oven until surface forms a lovely rubbery skin. Yummy!

Basque Tart/Pastel Vasco

This cake is originally from the Basque region of France and nowadays it is popular in the Spanish Basque region as well.

The dish goes back to the 17th century when it was made with almonds and stuffed with fruit or jam. Have a go at topping it with the Basque cross as a symbol of the region and it looks pretty too.

The Basque cross or lauburu (lau = four; buru = head) is a very old mythological symbol that represents the sun – a good omen which appears over many front doors, carved in stone, and is also used as a motif to decorate furniture, boxes, tombstones and jewellery.

Ingredients

• A tin of Cherry Pie Filling

The pastry:
• 125g unsalted butter
• 100g caster sugar
• 1 whole free-range egg
• 1 free-range egg yolk
• 225g plain flour
• ½ teaspoon baking powder
• 1 free-range egg, beaten to glaze

The filling:
• 300ml full-fat milk
• 1 vanilla pod, split and seeds scraped
• 4 free-range egg yolks
• 50g caster sugar
• 25g plain flour
• 2 teaspoons cornflour

Method

The pastry:
1. Beat the butter and sugar together until creamy and fluffy.
2. Beat in the egg and egg yolk, add the flour and baking powder.
3. Bring together to a dough and knead briefly until smooth, then shape into a disc and chill for 30 minutes.

The filling:
4. Heat the milk in a pan with the vanilla pod and seeds until almost boiling.
5. Beat the egg yolks and sugar together until fluffy then add the flours and beat until smooth.
6. Pour over the milk and mix together, then return the pan over a low heat and cook until you have a very thick, smooth mixture.
7. Spoon into a bowl, cover with cling film and leave to cool completely.

Combining pastry and filling:
8. Cut off a piece of pastry about 50g in weight to use to make

cont.

the lauburu (Basque Cross).

9. Divide the rest of the pastry into a third and two thirds.

10. Roll out the bigger bit and use to line the base and sides of a 25cm deep, loose-bottomed cake tin.

11. Spoon the cold cream filling into the tin, then clot spoonfuls of cherry filling over the top.

12. Roll out the smaller piece of pastry and cover the cherry filling, trimming away any excess and crimping the sides of the pastry together.

13. Roll out the last bit of pastry and cut out the Basque cross or just little shapes.

14. Brush the top of the pastry with the beaten egg, top with the cross or shapes, then glaze again.

15. Chill while you heat the oven to 180ºC/350ºF/gas 4

16. Bake the tart for 35-45 minutes until golden brown.

17. Leave to cool in the tin before releasing and serving.

Chocolate Truffles

Restaurants serve a dainty square of minted chocolate on the saucer beside your coffee but for a special occasion dinner at home you want something a bit more special. This is where homemade truffles come into their own. Everyone has a recipe for these little balls of delight, don't they? No? Well, here's one.

I can't remember if this came from one of my aunts, or from a friend whom I used to drop in to on a regular basis when the trials of young motherhood drove me out to seek adult company. With one child in the big pram and the other in the shopping basket underneath we bowled along the road to Christine's where a cup of coffee, her latest baking masterpiece and a good old natter would be waiting. Those were the days!

Ingredients

- 8 ounces of chocolate (good quality, 62% cacao or higher), chopped into small pieces
- ½ cup of double cream
- 1 teaspoon of vanilla extract or other flavourings such as sherry, rum, brandy, cinnamon etc.

Truffle coatings:
- cocoa powder, coconut or finely chopped almonds

Cocoa has a history dating back more than 4,000 years in Mexico and Central America. Chocolate, of which cacao is the basis, was introduced to Europe by the Spaniards, and by the mid-17th century was a popular beverage. A 1 kg bar of chocolate requires about 300 to 600 beans, depending on cocoa content.

Method

1. In a small saucepan bring the cream to a simmer.
2. If using an alternative to vanilla, stir desired flavourings in with the cream.
3. Place the chocolate in a bowl.
4. Pour the cream over the chocolate, add the vanilla (if using), and allow to stand for a few minutes.
5. Stir until smooth.
6. Allow to cool, then place in the refrigerator for two hours.
7. Using a teaspoon roll out balls of the mixture. Roll quickly in your hands as the heat of your hands will cause it to melt.
8. Place on a baking sheet lined with greaseproof paper and put in refrigerator overnight.
9. Take out and roll in cocoa powder, coconut or finely chopped almonds.
10. Keep in refrigerator until required, then wow your guests.

Maree Todd MSP's Controversial Tablet

Ingredients

This is the tablet recipe that caused a bit of a storm in the media and on social media when Maree gave three batches of her tablet to a summer camp for young people with experience of being in care. Unionists thought it inappropriate a Government Minister should encourage obesity just days after the government announced a crackdown on sugary foods. Maree made the tablet to show the children she cared.

Maree's tablet recipe was given to her by Elizabeth Fraser from Helmsdale. Maree feels one of the lovely things about sharing recipes, is that you think about who they came from each time you cook.

A traditional Scottish sweet, this is a treat not an everyday sweet.

- 2 lbs sugar
- 4 ozs butter
- 1 cup milk
- 1 can condensed milk
- 1 small teaspoon vanilla extract

Maree believes beating is the key to her tablet, which gives a great texture and seems to make it turn out right whether it is lightly over or underdone – it's a great trick, avoiding the need for sugar thermometers.

Method

1. Melt sugar, half butter and milk in a large pan and bring to the boil.
2. Add condensed milk and rest of butter, and bring to boil again.
3. Boil for 10-20 minutes, stirring frequently. (Don't worry if it catches a bit, it is usually retreivable, just adds to the colour, but don't wander off and hang out the washing or anything!)
4. It is ready when the colour changes to a golden caramel and the nature of the boil changes too – it goes from frothy/foamy to plopping like lava (all very scientific!).
5. You can test at this point if you want – drop a bit of mix into a cup of cold water and it should form a soft ball of toffee.
6. Take it off the heat and add the vanilla.
7. Beat for 4-5 minutes using electric beaters on medium setting – you will see it start to look grainy and a more set pattern appears.
8. Pour into a buttered tin and leave it to cool a bit. Cut while still warm. Enjoy!

Green Tomato and Apple Chutney

As every tomato grower knows, there are always the ones that won't ripen. Don't compost or bin them, make chutney out of them.

It's important to use all our home-grown vegeatables and encourage the growth of more as vegetable cultivation in Scotland has declined dramatically with substantially fewer varieties of home-grown vegetables now than in 1835. This is due to the high cost of glasshouses and of heating them and the need for seasonal labour. As a result many previously grown vegetables are now imported, either from south of the border, or from Europe, or much further afield. This explains why there are rumours of shortages after Brexit when the costs associated with leaving the EU will be felt in foodstuffs as well as elsewhere.

Ingredients

- 1kg green tomatoes
- 1kg sharp cooking apples
- ½ kg onions
- 100g raisins
- 100g sultanas
- Heaped teaspoon ground ginger
- large teaspoon pepper corns
- 1 tablespoon dry mustard powder
- 500ml vinegar (either malt or wine)
- 350g brown sugar
- 1 teaspoon salt.

Method

1. Skin the tomatoes. Putting them into boiling water for about 5 minutes then plunging them into ice water makes them much easier to skin.
2. Chop them into small bits.
3. Core and chop the apples.
4. Peel and finely chop the onions.
5. Put all the ingredients into a large strong pan. Stir well and bring slowly to a boil. Stir till the sugar has dissolved then simmer gently until it reaches setting point when a little is dropped into cold water.
6. Stir from time to time to prevent mixture from sticking to the pan.
7. When cooked pour into clean warmed jars and cover.
8. Keep in a cool place.

Traditional African Relish

A tasty and easily made accompaniment that goes with most savoury dishes and even perks up a plain salad.

Originally made in the local villages all over East Africa. It's now enjoyed by all the communities, African, Asian, Arab and European.

Scotland's involvement in African countries was significant with many staying decades and involved in commerce, as teachers and engineers, medical professionals, missionaries, and in cultural areas. Many of those Scots also fought for the independence of their adopted second homes.

Since the independence of the United States in 1776, 61 other British colonies have fought for and gained their independence, seventeen of them in Africa. Not one has returned to UK rule.

Ingredients

- Equal numbers of ripe tomatoes and onions.
- Salt to taste.
- A small pinch of chopped fresh chilli. Don't use chilli powder. It can become too hot.
- A little chopped fresh coriander if you like it.

Method

1. Chop the tomatoes and onions into small chunks.
2. Put both into a bowl and mix well.
3. Leave the mixture to sit for about five minutes and you will see a little liquid start to collect at the bottom of the bowl.
4. It's a good idea to taste a little bit of the liquid so you will know how much salt to add.
5. Cover the bowl and leave to sit for about an hour before serving. It lets the flavour develop.
6. Add the chilli and mix well just before serving.

The relish is normally served in a bowl and everyone helps themselves.

Wholegrain Mustard

With some things like cooked ham I like a wholegrain mustard and used to buy it in decent sized jars from Costco but they stopped stocking them and the tiny jars in most stores seemed overpriced - an obvious added margin item.

So I starting looking for recipes and settled on my own version. It is easy to make once you source the mustard seeds from one of the companies that supply mail order if your local whole food shop does not stock them. This recipe makes 2 good sized jars and keeps for several months in the fridge.

The Romans were probably the first to experiment with the preparation of mustard, now, as a cream or as individual seeds, mustard is used widely in cuisine, making it one of the most popular and widely used spices and condiments in the world.

Ingredients

- 100g yellow mustard seeds
- 100g black mustard seeds
- 250ml of wine, cider or white balsamic vinegar or mix of choice
- ½ tablespoon of choice – Irn Bru, or Dry Vermouth (latter stirred, never shaken – this is a stir it up cookbook!)
- juice of half a lemon or lime
- ½ teaspoon ground sea salt
- ½ teaspoon ground black pepper
- ½ teaspoon allspice

Method

1. Add the mustard seeds to a bowl with the vinegar.
2. Stir and cover with cling film and leave overnight for the seeds to soak up the liquid.
3. Place in food processor and add the remaining ingredients and blitz to required consistency.
The yellow seeds break down and the black seeds tend to remain mostly whole.
4. Place into clean jars and store in the fridge

Zanzibar Coffee

Arabica, the first known coffee originated in Africa where it's history can be traced back centuries to the ancient forests on the Ethiopian plateau. Long before arriving in Europe in the 16th century it was being enjoyed all over Africa. This recipe is a favourite with the Zanzibari people.

Zanzibar, home to humans for at least 20,000 years, by the 19th century was the centre of the Arab slave trade. It came under pressure from the UK to abolish its slave trade, with a threatened blockade of the island. leading, in 1890, to it becoming a protectorate of Britain. This lasted until 1963 when the Protectorate was terminated and in 1964 after the Zanzibar Revolution, it merged with mainland Tanganyika, now known as the United Republic of Tanzania, within which Zanzibar remains a semi-autonomous region.

Ingredients

- 6 cups water
- 6 cardamom pods
- 6 heaped teaspoons ground coffee
- 1 teaspoon ground ginger
- 1 teaspoon ground cardamom
- Sugar to taste

Method

1. Bring the water with the cardamom pods to the boil and simmer for 5 minutes.
2. Add the coffee and stir well.
3. Return the mixture to the boil and simmer for 3 minutes
4. Add the ginger and cardamom powder and simmer for another minute.
5. Strain into cups and serve with sugar.

You can adapt the spices to your own taste.

Fresh Mint Margaritas

This is a quick and easy cocktail to get a party going with tangy iced mint margaritas. Or it can be a really refreshing cocktail to help you unwind in the evening after a hard day's work.

Margaritas are thought to originate in Mexico (margarita is Spanish for daisy), with its main ingredient being tequila. The drink is served shaken with ice, blended with ice, or without ice, with freshly squeezed lime juice as the key ingredient. Rub the rim of the glass with a lime slice to make the salt stick to it and then roll in salt. Although served in a variety of glasses many stick with the margarita glass, a variant of the classic champagne coupe. Whatever glass the drink is served in, it probably came to us via America's cultural explosion in the UK or from those in the colonies.

Ingredients

- ½ cup chopped mint leaves
- ½ teaspoon salt
- 4 cups crushed ice
- 1½ cups good-quality tequila
- 1 cup freshly squeezed lime juice (from about 8 limes)
- 1 cup Triple Sec

1. In the bottom of a large (2-quart) pitcher, crush together mint and salt, pressing with the back of a wooden spoon.
2. Add ice.
3. Add tequila, lime juice, and Triple Sec, stirring vigorously.
4. Serve in short tumblers or wine glasses.
5. Relax and enjoy.

Banana Punch

A cold glass of refreshing punch really brightens any meal. It's nice to serve a crisp beverage like this that's more spectacular than plain juice. With bananas, orange juice and lemonade, it can add tropical flair to a grey Scottish winter day.

The origins of punch are lost in the mists of history but there is a theory that in the 17th-century an English sailor on his way to India mixed medicinal brandy from the ship's store, or more likely rum from the sailor daily ration, with water and a few ingredients obtained whilst on shore. By the 1660s, English sailors had spread punch from its origins in the Indian Ocean to the Caribbean, where it's been the characteristic drink of the region ever since.

Ingredients

- 6 medium ripe bananas
- 1 can (12 ounces) frozen orange juice concentrate, thawed
- ¾ cup thawed lemonade concentrate
- 3 cups warm water, divided
- 2 cups sugar, divided
- 1 can (46 ounces) pineapple juice, chilled
- 3 bottles (2 litres each) lemon-lime soda, chilled
- orange slices, optional

Method

1. In a blender, cover and process the bananas, orange juice and lemonade until smooth.
2. Remove half of the mixture and set aside.
3. Add 1½ cups warm water and 1 cup sugar to blender; blend until smooth.
4. Place in a large freezer container.
5. Repeat with remaining banana mixture, water and sugar; add to container.
6. Cover and freeze until solid.
7. One hour before serving, remove punch base from the freezer.
8. Just before serving, place in a large punch bowl.
9. Add pineapple juice and soda; stir until well blended.
10. Garnish with orange slices if desired.

Dawa Sundowner

Dawa is Medicine in Swahili, so when somebody asks you what you are drinking you can confidently tell them that you're taking your medicine.

Sundowners are cocktails consumed at sunset. The classic sundowner is Gin and Tonic, a drink originally introduced by the armed forces of the British East India Company in the early 19th century in India but which soon became a staple mix throughout the empire. In the 1700s a Scottish doctor discovered that quinine – a key ingredient in tonic water – was effective in treating and preventing malaria. For this reason, despie quinine's bitter and nasty flavour, it became widely consumed in tropical regions throughout the empire to keep malaria at bay. It was then made more palatable by mixing it with water, sugar, lime and gin. The G and T was born.

Ingredients

- 2 teaspoons white sugar or 1 tablespoon brown sugar
- 2 ounces vodka
- crushed ice cube
- 1 whole lime, quartered, with skin on
- ¾ cup of lime juice
- 1 Dawa stick (or wooden honey stick) twisted in creamed honey, or 2 tablespoons of honey

Method

1. Put lime and sugar into a whisky tumbler.
2. Crush limes slightly.
3. Add ice, and pour in the vodka.
4. Add lime juice.
5. At this point, you twist a Dawa stick into some honey and add the stick to the drink. A wooden honey stick or another type of stick twisted in honey will also work.
6. Muddle limes with Dawa or honey stick. The more you crush the limes into the mixture and stir with the honey stick, the sweeter your Dawa will taste.

Ounces to grams weight conversions
(all are approximate)

1 oz	30g	9 oz	255g
2 oz	60g	10 oz	280g
3 oz	90g	11 oz	310g
4 oz	110g	12 oz	340g
5 oz	140g	13 oz	370g
6 oz	170g	14 oz	400g
7 oz	200g	15 oz	425g
8 oz	225g	1 lb	450g

Liquid /dry conversions
3 teaspoons = 1 tablespoon   1 tablespoon = ½oz = 14.3grams
2tablespoons=1fl oz = 30ml
1 tablespoon = ½fl oz = 3 teaspoons = 15ml = 15cc
1 cup = 8 fl ozs = ½ pint = 16 tablespoons = 237ml

Oven temperature conversions

Fahrenheit	Celsius	Gas Mark	Description
250º F	130º C	½	Very cool
275º F	140º C	1	Very cool
300ºF	150ºC	2	Cool
325ºF	165ºC	3	Warm
350ºF	177ºC	4	Moderate
375ºF	190ºC	5	Moderrate
400ºF	200ºC	6	Moderately hot
425ºF	220ºC	7	Hot
450ºF	230ºC	8	Hot
475ºF	245ºC	9	Hot
500ºF	260ºC	10	Very hot